IMAGINATIVE WRITING
KEY STAGE 2 / SCOTTISH LEVELS C–E

Scholastic WRITING Workshop

C000156936

Writing
PROJECTS

GILL FRIEL
& SUE ELLIS

Published by Scholastic Ltd,
Villiers House,
Clarendon Avenue,
Leamington Spa,
Warwickshire CV32 5PR
Text © 1995 Gill Friel and Sue Ellis
© 1995 Scholastic Ltd

5 6 7 8 9 0   2 3 4

Authors
Gill Friel and Sue Ellis

Editor
Kate Banham

Assistant Editor
Sophie Jowett

Series Designer
Joy White

Designer
Sue Stockbridge

Illustrations
Ray and Corinne Burrows

Cover illustration
Frank James

Designed using Aldus Pagemaker

British Library Cataloguing-in-Publication Data
A catalogue record for this book is
available from the British Library.

ISBN 0 590 53467 X

Scholastic WRITING Workshop

Contents

Every effort has been made to trace the copyright holders for the works reproduced in this book and the publishers apologise for any inadvertent omissions.

The authors would like to thank the children of St Patrick's Primary School, Kilsyth, Killermont Primary School, Bearsden, and Fintry Primary School, Fintry, who helped in the development of these writing ideas.

Scholastic
IMAGINATIVE WRITING
Workshop

Scholastic WRITING Workshop

Chapter One

INTRODUCTION

TEACHING IMAGINATIVE WRITING

If we enable children to tell us what they know and care about, if we value their attempts to communicate and believe in their progress through the reading and writing of real stories, then we might find... that we have real writers sharing their stories with us. (Brigid Smith, 1992, in After Alice)

This resource has been developed for teachers who want to ensure that the imaginative writing requirements of the English curriculum are delivered in a way that:
• inspires the children with a love of story-telling and writing;
• teaches specific skills and strategies to improve the quality of writing and presentation;
• is responsive to children's different needs.

The importance of imaginative writing

When children create their *own* stories, they are empowered; they become the experts on the setting, characters and plot, and are freed from having to relate and respond to anyone else's reality. Telling stories can become a form of free play; the child is in charge and can manipulate the characters, action and outcome.

As they invent and tell imaginary stories, children learn how to use language to describe and sequence their ideas. They feel the power of language to 'story' ideas and they experience the pleasure of sharing these and of having their work read and appreciated by others.

Children as story-tellers

Conversations in any school dining hall confirm that children tell stories all the time. How the dog got lost, why their mum was cross or what they did last night all become stories as they set the scene, introduce characters and describe events. Some are better story-tellers than others, but all tell stories willingly and spontaneously.

Children also come to school full of the stories they have heard from others. Family and friends, television and video programmes, games and, of course, books provide a rich cultural experience that feeds the imagination.

Writing in the classroom

When teachers create classroom conditions in which children can use the story-telling skills evident in their play and conversation, they are freed from having to motivate children to write. Teacher and child can explore together the craft of story-telling and writing.

When the children know their stories are important, they think and act like writers. They plan, re-draft and edit their work because they themselves recognise that it is necessary. Their sense of ownership and of audience drives their desire to tell their stories well.

Teaching writing

Successful teachers foster children's belief in themselves as story-tellers and writers. They recognise that extended writing projects, in which children live the process from initial ideas, through the re-drafting stages to final publication, provide a powerful way to ensure that their children feel and act like writers.

Successful teachers also have a good understanding of writing and of how writers work. They are familiar with specific techniques and strategies, and encourage children to use those that are appropriate. They are skilled at working with children as writers and know when discussion will help and when they need to concentrate and work alone. They are also skilled at planning with children's needs in mind, and the sequence and structure of their writing lessons ensure that children think about, and are supported in, the craft of writing and story-telling in a variety of ways.

Finally, successful teachers have a good understanding of children and are sensitive to their needs as writers. They are observant and analytical of the writing produced, but their teaching and comments are focused primarily on the writer, not the product. They accept that, while they might introduce and teach specific skills and strategies, only the writer may choose to apply them, so effective teaching must involve exploring why and how young writers make choices and craft a story.

WRITING PROJECTS

This volume contains:
• ten writing projects in which children invent and craft their own extended stories;
• a presentation chapter which details effective ways to present and publish work, enabling children to develop an awareness and appreciation of audience.

The writing projects

The writing projects enable the whole class to engage in individual and collaborative writing. They cover a range of genres and vary in length and focus, allowing the teacher to choose those which best fit the needs and interests of the children and the time available.

The extended nature of the projects allows children to 'live' with a story for long enough to become emotionally involved with it and committed to writing it well. When children are given the space and time to think, feel and behave like writers, they discover their own recipes for success and begin to celebrate writing as both a process and a product.

Each project suggests original publishing formats, designed to entice both adults and children to read them. Seeing others read and enjoy their work boosts the young writer's sense of audience, ownership and self-esteem.

The projects have been carefully structured to provide inspiration and support for young writers. They offer detailed lesson plans that have been designed to create contexts which teach children how to write and about the writing process. The writing projects:

- engage children's imagination;
- allow the children time to live with and become emotionally committed to their stories;
- provide the children with both the support and freedom to decide how to tell their stories;
- ensure that writing is a pleasurable and purposeful activity;
- provide feedback and a sense of audience throughout the writing process.

Children will learn to:

- use language effectively and economically;
- create and portray characters;
- describe and use setting and place;
- develop a range of story structures;
- take account of audience needs;
- draw on their own experiences as readers to improve their writing;
- develop techniques for planning, drafting and re-drafting their work;
- write for different purposes and audiences;
- read and learn from each other's work;
- collaborate with others, learning to use and become a 'critical friend'.

The structure and sequence of *Writing Projects* activities

The structure and sequence of the activities for each writing project ensure that each session acts as a springboard for the next. The activities provide the necessary focus to help young writers generate new ideas and develop existing ones. They help teachers and children to change the pace of work, while maintaining the project's momentum. There are opportunities to reflect on work done so far and to plan ahead. The projects encourage children to work both alone and with others, and also to discuss their work in formal and informal situations. This encourages familiarity with a range of work patterns, and it helps children to understand new ideas and to consolidate old ones.

How do the projects relate to activities in *Aspects of the Craft of Writing*?

In learning to write, children need to control their own stories, finding their own problems and solutions. The writing projects encourage children to think and behave like writers. Children will develop and apply many skills, techniques and strategies central to the writer's craft. They will learn how writers think and behave and how they integrate, select, reflect and plan. Thus, the writing projects help children to learn about writing and the process of writing in an integrated and holistic way.

However, children also need opportunities to focus on specific aspects, and their attendant skills, techniques and strategies in an isolated way. *Aspects of the Craft of Writing* provides activities that highlight particular strategies associated with specific aspects. This allows for tightly focused teaching of specific skills, techniques and strategies, where appropriate.

The books complement each other. They allow teachers to be creative, flexible and analytical in their approach, choosing writing projects or activities from *Aspects of the Craft of Writing* as appropriate.

Presentation chapter

If children are to take a pride in their own and others' writing, the work must be presented in an eye-catching and exciting way.

Children's attitudes to their work will be influenced by how others respond to it. When friends and relatives show obvious delight in the finished product, it reinforces the pleasure of story-telling and the children's sense of audience, authorship and achievement.

Each writing project suggests specific formats for publishing the story. The presentation chapter gives ideas for teaching children about:

- creating front and back covers and prelims;
- the shape, layout and function of illustrations;
- calligraphy, illuminated letters and borders;
- promotion of the books they have written.

	Collaborative demands and outcome	Planning	Drafting
The Magic Box	Easy demands; individual outcome.	Initial ideas; sequencing.	Beginnings.
Animal Adventures	Low demands; individual or paired outcome.	Use of ideas sheet.	
Top Dog at Last	Easy demands; individual outcome.	Starting with character.	Re-reading and reviewing work.
The Monsters' Feast	High demands; some joint writing; individual outcome.	Using drama to plan and sequence ideas.	Joint drafting/ re-drafting.
Pirate Adventure	Medium/high demands; some joint writing; joint outcome.		Balance and consistency; collaborative (re-)drafting.
Castles in the Air	Medium/low demands; individual outcome.	Planning – event that drives story.	Conferencing with teacher.
Star Myth	Medium demands; collaborative story-telling; individual outcome.	Story-mapping.	
True Stories	Medium demands; individual outcome.	Skeleton list of main events to be elaborated upon.	
Adventure at Seabay School	High demands; joint outcome.	Strongly supported.	Collaborative composing and re-drafting.
The Bully	High demands; collaborative planning; individual writing; joint outcome.	Highly structured.	

Characterisation	Place and setting	Structure	Audience/ celebration	Public... forma...
		Beginnings; story sequencing.	Review by peers and one other person important to the child.	A4-sized book.
Using real people/pets; character study; viewpoints.		Endings; titles; sequencing short stories.	Child's choice.	Short story book.
Through appearance; using research.		Sad to happy structure; narrator as storyteller; endings.	Story reading at home; child invites audience.	Children select best format.
Through speech; appearance.	Using place description to create mood.	Using letters, dialogue and menus to move story forward.	Read aloud to younger and/or older children.	Shaped zigzag books.
Inventing rounded characters.	Straight descriptions of place.	Cliff-hangers; prologues; endings; titles.	Read aloud to peer groups.	Serial story in A3 'Big Book' format.
	Straight descriptions of place.	Fairy story beginnings; divisions and story layout.	Read aloud to younger children in the school.	3D castle books.
			Peer evaluation	Big class book and story tape.
Creating a self-portrait.		Writing a prologue.	A well-known adult.	Large sheet of card with photograph.
Creating a balanced group of characters.	Atmospheric description of secret place.	Story beginnings; cliff-hangers; turning points; chapters.	Peer reviews.	Customised school jotter written by group of four.
Structured support sheet.		Prologue; turning points; chapters.	Peer evaluation and review; loan scheme.	A4-sized flip-over book written in pairs.

CLASSROOM MANAGEMENT

Selecting a project: where to start

The type of stories children find easy to write depends on the type of stories they have experienced as readers, and this will vary within a class. Many projects begin with collaborative work in which children generate ideas and storylines. In this way, readers with more enthusiasm, knowledge and experience support those with less.

Each project has a different focus, makes different demands on the writing skills of the writers, and has a different time-span. A short summary of the content and focus, including key areas of support can be found at the start of each project and this information is summarised in the project summary chart on pages 8–9.

Teachers will need to select the project that offers the focus and support that best fits the needs and interests of the children in their class and the amount of time available. Inspiration and creativity are infectious and the projects are most effective when they involve the whole class, rather than one or two groups. Projects with the whole class mean that the children benefit from seeing and responding to a wider range of ideas than can be generated within a single group. They also provide an opportunity for children to work with a wider range of partners. For the teacher, they simplify time-consuming aspects of forward planning and collecting and organising resources, freeing them to focus on the task of observing, teaching and working alongside the children.

The projects are not star-rated or presented in a strict order of difficulty because there are too many factors that influence what any child may find difficult. Children's experience of reading and listening to a particular type of story, their previous writing experience, their experience of working collaboratively, supporting each other and presenting their ideas to others will all influence whether they find a particular writing project easy or hard.

Projects such as 'The Magic Box' or 'Castles in the Air' draw on the sort of fairy story structure and ideas with which most children are likely to be familiar. These have highly-structured, collaborative activities and therefore often make good starting points for a class

which is unused to sustaining a storyline over several sessions.

Obviously, teachers will want to ensure that, over the course of a year, children are not always required to write the same type of story. When a teacher has completed one writing project with the class, she will know which of the remaining projects to tackle next.

Planning time for the projects

To allow the ideas to develop continuity and momentum, it is recommended that the writing projects are treated as concentrated 'blocks' of work. When too much time elapses between writing sessions, the children become demotivated; they forget where they have got to, lose the enthusiasm built up in the previous session and the end product is a long time coming. Flexible timetabling that allows children 3–5 sessions per week for a project is ideal. Those subjects which miss out during the project can be given additional time before and after it. Both teachers and children will appreciate that one, concentrated project in which children beg to be allowed to write, is a far more effective and enjoyable situation than several shorter activities in which unwilling children are cajoled and pushed into producing something on paper.

Drafting, editing and publishing

All the projects assume that children are familiar with the processes of drafting, editing and publishing work. If the teacher cannot be sure that all the children in the class have met these key ideas before, it is a good idea to introduce drafting as a class lesson before children start work on a particular project. The concepts and skills of editing and publishing can be introduced as children reach the relevant stage of a project.

Explain re-drafting by telling the children that often, when a writer first starts to write a story, the most important thing is to get the story down on paper in the most exciting, sad or funny way possible, depending on what sort of story it is. At this stage, the writer is not too concerned about neatness, handwriting, spelling or punctuation.

Show the children a piece of writing that you have re-drafted yourself. Perhaps it is a report, part of a forecast of work or a letter. There is no need to allow close scrutiny of the contents, but point out that everyone develops their own code for re-drafting and that all writers (even teachers) produce rough drafts. It is important for children to see adults as writers – too often they believe that writing is an exercise that only exists in school and is only done siting in class.

Explain that, while writing, writers often find they have to re-read a script regularly to collect their thoughts and keep the narrative flowing. As they read, they frequently make alterations; they cross out sections or re-write them using stars, arrows or numbers to show where the new passage should fit in. Show the children the system you personally use, and ask them which, if any, they have used in the past and which they may use in the project ahead.

Conferencing

In all the projects, there will be times when the teacher sits with an individual child, or a group of children to talk about a story that is under way. These times are important, not only because the teacher is engaged in directly addressing individual needs, but also because such situations provide opportunities for the teacher to model how to be a good writing partner.

In conducting a writing conference, therefore, the teacher needs to be seen as another, more experienced writer, who is there to listen to problems, help the writer overcome difficulties, spell out the options and give advice. The teacher should sit with the child or group in a peaceful place. It is important to keep the conference requirements quite simple and not be too ambitious.

It is essential that each story makes sense, but the rest of the discussion should be guided by what the child says about his writing, the story he has to tell, and where the teacher thinks the needs lie.

During the conference, ask questions that teach *you* about the child. To help you understand the child as a writer, you may need, for example, to find out how the ideas for the story developed or which parts particularly engender feelings of pride.

It is important to ask the child to evaluate the strengths and weaknesses of the story and to work through this evaluation to make the teaching points. Ensure that you make an opportunity to tell the child something you particularly like about what they have written, and why. At the end of the conference, send the child away with *one* thing to think about and to make changes in the light of this.

This way of working ensures that the child not only feels that the work has been taken seriously by the teacher, but that he understands *why* some changes may need to be made and *why* some bits of the story work so well. It scaffolds the process of self-evaluation and ensures that children make changes to their writing because they understand what they need to do to make it more effective, not because the teacher has told them to. Some children may want to return to you after re-writing parts of the story, so ensure that your classroom organisation allows for this.

Depending on the stage the story has reached, the writing conference might include some of the following activities/discussion openers:
- The child reads through the story with you.
- Ask the child what he thinks is the best part of the story, and why.
- Ask the child what he thinks the others will like best about the story, and why.
- Say something positive about what you liked in the story.
- Discuss any parts which need clarifying. Mark these with an asterisk.
- Comment on how the child has introduced and used the characters and place. Ask questions to find out what decisions the child made and what criteria they were based on.
- Identify one aspect that may need further work and ask the child to comment on it.

Finally, with some children, you may also want to consider the spelling and punctuation. Does the punctuation help the story to read well? Go through and elicit corrections from the child. With some children it may be enough just to do this for the first part of the story, with others you may need to go through the whole story, getting the child to identify and explain punctuation and spelling decisions. Emphasise that punctuation and spelling must be correct if others are to read and understand the story. You may choose to underline a few spellings that can be easily found in dictionaries or give correct spellings yourself. The approach to spelling and punctuation will be individualised, as different children will be best helped by different responses.

Children who have difficulty in making the story flow can sometimes be helped by re-reading their work at regular intervals, or by having someone else read it aloud to them. Some children are helped if the teacher or another child writes a few connecting parts, although obviously this must be done sensitively – the child must retain ownership and responsibility for the story as a whole. However, writing with other people is an excellent way to learn and it leaves such children with a complete story that they may not have managed alone at this stage.

Likewise, children with serious spelling difficulties may be helped by the teacher copying out the story while the child watches. Together you can pick out simple words as you go and discuss these spellings. Throughout, it is important that children realise that correct punctuation and spelling help readers to read with understanding.

Organising the class

Most of the projects involve children working with a writing partner. It takes time to establish working relationships and partners need to know about each other's work in order to give informed advice. For these reasons, it is important that children keep the same partner for all the 'paired' sessions within a project. It is best if children are allowed to choose a friend, or someone they will feel comfortable working with, rather then be assigned a partner by the teacher, although, obviously, the teacher must retain the right to veto some pairings!

Children should be encouraged to select different writing partners for each new project, however, since this ensures that they work with a range of people in the class and benefit from different working relationships and the different viewpoints, feedback and advice they generate.

Collecting and organising the work

Schools will already have most of the resources required for the writing projects. It is often useful for children to be given:
• files in which they can keep loose pieces of writing for future reference;
• drafting notebooks in which they can record ideas, make notes and first drafts. This ensures that none of the work gets lost and the notebooks can provide interesting evidence of any changes which the child has made to the story and the ways in which a child's writing has developed.

Notebooks can provide a good focus for discussion and review, during which the teacher will learn about the child and the child will learn about writing.

Choosing and organising resources for publication

Children must have good quality resources if they are to take pride in the presentation of their work. For most projects, they will need:
• good quality paper on which to write out or mount their writing;
• colouring pens and pencils (both thick and thin) for illustrations (these should work and be easy to use);

• a variety of shapes and sizes of paper suitable for writing and for illustrations;
• tiny pieces of collage materials, chosen to inspire the children – sequins, netting, gold and silver foil, shiny paper, fabrics, wallpaper samples, wrapping paper, etc;
• PVA glue and spreaders.

Each table of children can be given responsibility for their own tray containing all the materials they need for the project they are working on. The plastic canisters in which photographic films are bought make excellent containers for the PVA glue and for individual collage materials.

The layout of the activities

The following information is given by icons at the start of each session:

Class organisation details whether the children will be working individually, in pairs, in larger groups, or as a class.

Time required gives a rough guide to how long each session may take. Obviously, this can only be a very rough guide and much will depend on individual teachers and classes.

Each session has been clearly laid out under the following headings:

Teaching content explains the main teaching objectives of each activity.

What you need details at a glance what resources are required for the session.

What to do explains exactly how to introduce and structure the lesson.

Using the books

Some of the children's books included in this *Scholastic Writing Workshop* can be used in conjunction with the writing projects to inspire ideas and provide good examples of genre. This is indicated on the writing project concerned and on the project summary chart. All the writing projects are accompanied by a list of books that teachers may find helpful to encourage the children to read, either during or after the project work.

Chapter Two
ASSESSMENT

ASSESSMENT

The writing projects allow teachers to observe and work with children on their writing over a period of time. This enables them to form a picture of each child that is informed by a rich variety of evidence. A good teacher assesses all the time she is teaching. She cannot help but notice and take account of:

• what children do;
• what children say about what they have done;
• what children find easy or difficult and can do only with help;
• what type of help is most useful;
• what the children particularly enjoy;
• what the children do not like and why;
• the work the children produce.

The difficulty in terms of assessment is in noting, and making detailed records of, the triumphs, difficulties and needs of each child. The danger is that the assessment and recording arrangements take so much time that the teacher's attention and energies are diverted from the most important purpose of assessment: that of analysing needs and providing learning activities and teaching input to develop each child's skills and understanding. It is, after all, the correspondence between the child's needs and the teaching input that determines the speed with which children progress.

General assessment and record-keeping photocopiable pages

A number of generic assessment and record-keeping pages are provided for the writing projects in this book. They are intended to link with, and complement, those in the *Aspects of the Craft of Writing* volume.

Writing Projects provides two photocopiable sheets that are intended as generic formative assessment and recording frameworks. It is expected that teachers will use and adapt these to suit their own needs and the policies of the school. If a particular framework is not successful in helping the teacher teach more effectively, it should be abandoned.

Class/group notes (page 16)

The class/group notes page provides a format for teachers to make informal notes, on a daily basis if necessary, to remind themselves of particular children who stood out during the

lesson and why. It is divided into two broad sections: 'process' and 'craft'. These are obviously not exclusive, but the division may help teachers to analyse where the general needs and strengths of the class lie. As teachers add comments to the class record over the course of a writing project, they will find that some names crop up frequently and others less frequently, if at all. It is often productive to consider why some children are not mentioned, if only so that the teacher can be sure that this is because their needs are being met rather than because they are being overlooked.

Individual project report (page 17)

The individual project report provides a framework for focusing on the achievements and needs of individual children. It is intended to help teachers analyse children's work with a view to identifying appropriate support or challenges in the future. It targets three important areas that the teacher must consider:

The child as a writer: this section can be completed during the project work. It includes information on what the child enjoyed or hated, found easy or hard. It allows the teacher to comment on what she has observed about the child's preferred strategies for planning, drafting and editing, as well as on the child's attitudes both during the writing process and when the story has been published and read.

Teacher comment on the story written: this section allows the teacher to use the 'craft aspects' framework to analyse how the child has chosen to tell the story - commenting on the strongest aspects of characterisation, setting or structure and on the nature and range of the writing strategies that have been used.

Teacher-child discussion: this section allows the teacher to record and comment on the child's evaluation and response to the teacher's observations and judgements. It assumes that teachers have discussed the project work with the child. There is a photocopiable sheet tailored for each writing project to help children to share and evaluate their work in discussion with various people. These help children to clarify and review their own feelings and opinions and can provide a useful basis for discussion with the class teacher.

Overall class record of activities: *Writing Projects* (page 18)

This is a record that can be passed on to the next year teacher to show which projects have already been covered by the class.

Scholastic
IMAGINATIVE WRITING
Workshop

When to use the individual assessments

Teachers must choose when it is appropriate to do an individual project report, and should not necessarily feel the need to do one for every child on every writing project. They may of course decide that they want to do this, perhaps when they have just inherited a class and do not know the children well. However, they could equally choose to target particular groups of children for particular projects, thus covering the whole class over a year.

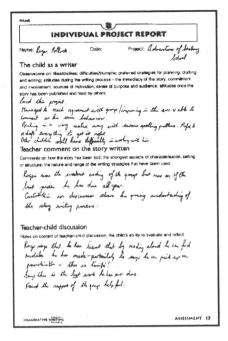

• It can prompt analytical self-evaluation – children often recognise strengths and weaknesses in someone else's work before they can recognise those same qualities in their own work.

• Children have to justify their opinions. This encourages them to be analytical but also promotes deep learning: the act of articulating and explaining ideas helps children to broaden, clarify and consolidate their understanding.

• It helps children to make reading–writing links, using their experience as readers to help them write effectively.

Providing feedback for the child

Neither of these formats is intended to provide specific comments or feedback for the child on how the story could be improved. In part, this is because the end of a project is too late for such advice which is most helpful during the writing process, while the children are making decisions and crafting the story. Each writing project provides for this sort of advice and support from both the teacher and writing partners during the work.

Once the projects have been published, the teacher's feedback to the children needs to celebrate their achievements and encourage them to share in the achievements of others.

Self-evaluation and peer evaluation

Self-evaluation and peer evaluation is integral to each writing project and to many of the activities in *Aspects of the Craft of Writing*. Self-evaluation is important because it helps children to become efficient, and effective learners.

• It helps to make children aware of what they know and what they can do.

• It provides a basis from which to analyse learning needs, monitor progress and to celebrate good work.

• It develops self-knowledge, confidence and self-esteem.

Peer evaluation provides an equally powerful tool for learning. It is important for several reasons.

• Some children are daunted by discussing the work of published authors, and are more willing to respond to writing that has been produced by someone they know.

Summative assessment

We recommend that teachers keep a portfolio of the work of each child. The portfolio might contain any or all of the following:

• published stories from the writing projects;
• examples of first and second drafts;
• evaluations and comments by the child;
• evaluations and comments by other readers, or people with whom the child worked;
• writing produced in response to the activities in *Aspects of the Craft of Writing*;
• writing review forms (see *Aspects of the Craft of Writing*, page 20) completed by the child and/or the teacher.

Teachers need to devise their own policy for what is included in the writer's portfolio. There are several options. They may decide to do any of the following:

• Devise a policy that pre-determines specific pieces of work to be included in each child's portfolio;

• Determine set 'portfolio review times' when either the teacher or the children review the contents and the balance of the portfolios, adding work as appropriate.

• Encourage children to consider adding items to the portfolios as they complete individual pieces of work.

Obviously, with the emphasis on formative assessment, teachers will find that over a period of time they have built up a detailed picture of each child and their characteristics as writers. They will find that a review of each child's portfolio and of their formative assessment notes provides ample evidence on which summative and evaluative reports can be written.

CLASS/GROUP NOTES

The process of writing

Sense of audience and purpose; confidence and willingness to develop story ideas, to work individually and collaboratively and to reflect on work; attitudes and strategies for planning, re-drafting, editing; reactions to publication.

Craft aspects

Characterisation   Setting   Structure

INDIVIDUAL PROJECT REPORT

Name: Date: Project:

The child as a writer

Observations on: likes/dislikes; difficulties/triumphs; preferred strategies for planning, drafting and editing; attitudes during the writing process – the immediacy of the story, commitment and involvement, sources of motivation, sense of purpose and audience; attitudes once the story has been published and read by others.

Teacher comment on the story written

Comments on how the story has been told; the strongest aspects of characterisation, setting or structure; the nature and range of the writing strategies that have been used.

Teacher-child discussion

Notes on content of teacher–child discussion; the child's ability to evaluate and reflect.

OVERALL CLASS RECORD OF ACTIVITIES: WRITING PROJECTS

Projects	Year3/P4	Year 4/P5	Year 5/P6	Year 6/P7
The magic box				
Animal adventures				
Top dog at last				
The monsters' feast				
Pirate adventure				
Castles in the air				
Star myth				
True stories				
Adventure at Seabay School				
The bully				

Scholastic WRITING Workshop

Chapter Three

THE MAGIC BOX

INTRODUCTION

Project description

In this project children write a fantasy adventure story in three chapters, centred around the idea of a magic box. The initial brainstorming of ideas is supported by a photocopiable sheet and is completed in pairs. Thinking time is built into the project to allow children to develop individual storylines and then tell their stories to writing partners.

A planning sheet helps children to organise their stories into three parts with a clear beginning, middle and end. They are asked to draft different ways of beginning the story and to discuss with their writing partner which opening to use. With a strong beginning and a clearly-outlined story plan, the children can develop and write their extended, imaginative stories.

The stories are then each evaluated by two reviewers, who write reviews which are placed in a specially made box which fits on the back of the book.

Why this context?

Children love fantasy adventures and this project gives them an opportunity to indulge in a real flight of fancy. The discussion between writing partners, along with the photocopiable sheets, supports children in generating initial story ideas and in selecting and organising their ideas. Telling the story to a writing partner helps the children to understand what the reader needs to know, as well as allowing them to rehearse the sequencing and structure of their story before they begin to commit it to paper.

This project also focuses attention on the different ways to begin stories and raises awareness of the importance of a good, strong opening.

Project organisation

The children begin by working in pairs to brainstorm ideas for their story, choosing the best of these to bring to a class discussion. They are given time to select their ideas individually before jotting down very brief story planning notes.

Individually, they are then asked to write two alternative story openings and to discuss with their writing partners which they prefer, and why. Once the beginning has been chosen, the children work individually to write and illustrate their stories.

Publication and presentation

The stories are written on to A4 paper and illustrations in a variety of sizes and shapes are added at appropriate points. The stories are read and reviewed by writing partners and by an adult who is important to the writer.

Books the children may find useful

Greenwitch by Susan Cooper (Penguin)
Last Slice of Rainbow by Joan Aiken (Penguin)
Through the Magic Mirror by Anthony Browne (Macmillan)
The Snow Maze by Jan Mark (Walker Books)
Mike's Magic Seeds by Alexander McCall Smith (Corgi)
The Mirrorstone by Michael Palin (Cape)

1

MAGIC IDEAS FOR THE MAGIC BOX

Teaching content
Generating and selecting ideas.

What you need
Photocopiable page 27, writing materials.

What to do
Tell the children that they are going to write a story about a magic box. Explain that they will be doing the initial brainstorming for story ideas in pairs, but that the actual planning and writing will be an individual task. The brainstorm activity encourages diversity of thought and at the end the children should have a massive range of ideas to draw on for their stories.

Organise the class into writing partners and give each pair a copy of photocopiable page 27. Read through the questions with the children and explain that they must try to find three different answers for each question. Explain that they can answer them in any order and that ideas should not be linked. Allow 10–15 minutes for this, then ask the children each to select one idea from the sheet and to bring this to a whole class discussion. Explain that during the discussion, children should listen for ideas that they can combine with theirs, or ideas that they prefer to their original choice. Emphasise that this is fine. Writers get ideas in many ways from many sources, and all writers change their ideas, sometimes more than once, before finally settling for the one on which they will base a particular story.

Give the children a few minutes to make their choice and then ask every child to read out his or her favourite idea and indicate the question to which it relates.

Explain that now children will have an evening's 'thinking time' before taking the next step towards writing a long, magical story. Tell them that published writers often change their minds many times before they begin writing, and some children may change their minds overnight about best ideas. Perhaps someone else in the class has given them a better idea and ideas are to be shared. Stories will develop very differently even if they have the same starting point. Many writers say they get their best ideas as they go off to sleep and sometimes get wonderful inspiration as they wake up in the morning. Encourage the children to become writers who 'sleep on' their ideas.

Explain that by tomorrow everyone should have thought out a story about a magic box. The story can be about other people or strange mythical creatures and the children themselves may be a part of the story if they choose.

2

PLANNING THE STORY
†–†† ⏱40

Teaching content
Planning and structuring the story.

What you need
Photocopiable page 27 (completed), photocopiable page 28 (optional), writing materials.

What to do
Explain that every story has characters to whom something happens – an event, a problem, a surprise... Give each child a copy of photocopiable page 28 and ask them to jot down answers to each of the questions. This

should help them to plan their story, incorporating their ideas from photocopiable page 27.

After 5–10 minutes ask the children to tell their stories to their writing partners. Explain that, quite often, people who have a good story in their heads assume that others know the story equally well and omit important background details. Partners must listen carefully to stories and, when they don't understand what is happening, must stop the story-teller and ask questions. In this way it becomes clear to the story-teller what must be included so that the story may be understood and enjoyed by the reader.

Through this process of 'telling', each child is given an opportunity to clarify and firm up the story ready for writing. A further night of 'sleeping on it' may lead to changes in the storyline but should also ensure that all the children have a story to write with a beginning, a middle and an end.

Encourage them to tell their stories to someone at home, which will help to further establish a clear storyline in their minds.

3

GOOD BEGINNINGS
††††–† ⏱45

Teaching content
Developing ideas about what makes an effective opening sentence.

What you need
Photocopiable page 29, writing materials.

What to do
Photocopiable page 29 gives examples of four different ways to begin a story. Discuss with the children how each opening differs and explain that any story can begin in these different ways. A writer must decide how to begin a story and these are only four examples of the many different choices that are available.

Arrange the children in groups of four and ask them to discuss which opening sentence they think makes the most exciting story opening. Remind them that a good beginning is one that grabs the reader's attention and demands that she read on! There is no correct answer, but in discussing ideas and opinions

the children are learning about what makes a good opening. After 5 minutes hold a brief class discussion, allowing the children to put forward the main points that emerged from their group discussions.

Next, ask individuals to choose two ways of starting a story and to write two beginnings, one in each style, for their own stories. Give about 10 minutes for this before asking partners to share what they have written. Pairs should discuss which opening they like best and why. In this way, help, advice and encouragement is given just at the point when story writing is about to begin and not at the end when it's too late. Writers may or may not begin their stories with the starting point favoured by their partners. A writer must have ownership of his own writing and so must make the final crucial decision alone.

4

WRITING THE STORY

Teaching content

Writing the story.

What you need

Writing materials, completed photocopiable pages 27 and 28, illustrated storybooks.

What to do

The children are now ready and prepared to write the story. They know how their story will begin and they know what will happen in it. In this session you will explain the organisation of time and materials and help the children to visualise the finished product.

There is a lot of information for the children to consider. However, it is important that before they begin writing, children know exactly how the story is to be illustrated and presented and that they have a clear overview of how the writing will progress.

Children are given a sense of control and independence through being allowed to make choices, yet the supportive and highly structured framework ensures that the classroom is not chaotic. The following points must be covered before children begin to write. Each of these aspects is elaborated upon in the presentation chapter if detailed guidance is needed.

In groups of four or five, ask the children to examine the illustrated storybooks. Ensure that some of them include a writer's dedication at the front. Draw attention to the following points:

Writer's dedication: Explain that some authors write a book with a particular person they love or admire in mind. They often indicate this in the dedication and it transforms the book into a precious gift. Ask children to think of someone to whom they would like to dedicate their

books. Explain that, after the story has been written, they will be making covers and title, contents and dedication pages for their books. The idea of writing as a gift sharpens the search for excellence and high standards during the writing and publishing processes.

Organisation of writing and illustrations: Note how the illustrations and writing are organised on a page to lend interest to a story. Point out that illustrations are not always contained within the same space or shape and that sometimes writing is arranged around, above, below or to the side of the illustration.

Large. illuminated letters: Draw attention to the storybooks that begin with beautiful illuminated letters and tell the children that they may also begin their books this way. Refer children to the calligraphy books for ideas.

New chapters: Show the children how new chapters are numbered and that each new chapter begins on a new page. Explain that they may divide the beginning, middle and end of their stories into chapters and that each chapter must begin on a new page. Sometimes new chapters are given a heading/title and children may do this if they choose.

Materials for writing and illustrating: If the children are experienced writers and have been taught several methods of book-making, then you may like to offer a choice of publication formats, including word processing. If they are less experienced then it is best to teach just one format. We suggest A4 lined paper with illustrations on plain paper stuck into place. These pages can be stapled when finished, preferably across the top or down the left-hand side.

Show the children where the A4 lined paper may be found. Make it clear which materials may be used for illustrating and where they can be found.

Explain when children will be given writing time over the next two or three days. Tell the children that writers sometimes take a break when they become tired of writing or need fresh inspiration. By allowing children to choose when they make illustrations or fancy borders for their books, you are offering them a breathing space. Over the next few days they can write and illustrate whenever they choose, but all publications must be completed on time.

Keep reminding the children of time over the next few days and circulate often enough to ensure that they are all making progress in their writing. Emphasise that, although illustrations are crucial in a finished publication, the main focus of this particular activity is the writing of the story and that it must be finished. Point out that published writers also have deadlines to meet.

FINAL PUBLICATION DETAILS

Teaching content
* How books are organised.
* Form and content of front page.

What you need
Illustrated storybooks, large sheet of paper, writing materials, art and collage materials, children's work, A4 card, A4 plain paper.

What to do
All the activities suggested here are elaborated upon in the presentation chapter if detailed guidance is needed.

When some children have finished writing and illustrating their stories, stop the class and explain the final stages of the project. Ask the children, in groups, to study the front covers and initial pages of the storybook exemplars you have chosen. Publications have slight variations but mostly follow the same basic rules. Elicit the following details from the children and write them on a large sheet of paper for permanent display as children finish their work.

Front cover
This has the:
* book title;
* author's name;
* illustrator's name;
* publisher's name.

The children will have to decide how to organise this information on the front page. If you are not using computers, remind the children to use rulers to keep their writing straight and show them how to block out letters roughly to ensure they are even and suitably sized. Point out that the style of lettering must also be consistent.

A border drawn round the front page will help the book to look professional and give it a 'finished' appearance. Encourage the children to make a rough sketch of the cover design

before committing it to a piece of A4 card. Explain that it is best to finish making the front cover before stapling it on to the writing, either across the top or down the left-hand side.

Title page
This also has the:
* book title;
* author's name;
* illustrator's name (often a small illustration is incorporated on this page).

Dedication page
If an author wishes to dedicate a book, this goes often on the back of the title page, together with a declaration of copyright and a date of publication. Ask children to find and

read some dedications and copyright statements. Encourage them to note how this information is laid out in different books and discuss how different sizes of print are used for different types of information. Only once children have done this, should they plan their own layout.

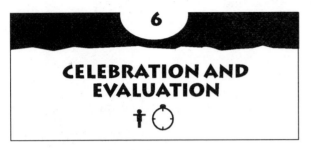

CELEBRATION AND EVALUATION

Teaching content
- Analytical self-evaluation.
- Teacher assessment.

What you need
Magic Box stories, photocopiable pages 30–32, scissors, glue, writing materials.

What to do
Now that the children have produced their extended stories they should be given an opportunity to celebrate their work and achievement in several different ways, with several different audiences. Give each author a copy of the magic box template on photocopiable page 30. Ask them to cut it out, to make it up and to stick it on to the back page of their publication. Photocopiable page 31 can be used for parents and peers to record their responses to and comments about a particular story. One half of the sheet should be given to a parent or adult reviewer, and the other half should be given to a schoolfriend of the author. The two sets of comments should be cut out, folded and placed in the magic box, thus providing two reviews of each book for future readers.

It is also important for the children to evaluate their own work, and photocopiable page 32, 'The Magic Box – Self-Evaluation', provides a format for this. You may find this page useful when you come to assess the writing; there is no point in looking at the writing without taking account of how the writer views it.

With younger or less experienced writers you may choose to read through the sheet with the child, explain what each question means and complete it together. Begin by listening carefully to the child's comments and build from the child's observations to the points that you would like to explore.

With older children, who are more confident in their writing and evaluation, you may choose to complete your own evaluation sheet independently of the child's evaluation, and then compare the two sets of comments.

MAGIC IDEAS FOR THE MAGIC BOX

What is magical about the box?

1. _____

2. _____

3. _____

Who hid the box?

1. _____

2. _____

3. _____

Why was the box hidden?

1. _____

2. _____

3. _____

Who found the box?

1. _____

2. _____

3. _____

Where was it found?

1. _____

2. _____

3. _____

PLANNING THE STORY

Who are the main characters?
What are they like?

Where does the story begin?
What happens to start the story off?

What happens next?

What happens in the end?
How does the story finish?

GOOD BEGINNINGS

◆ There are lots of different ways to start a story. The examples on this page show some possible openings.

Starting with a mystery and a place:

In the middle of the deep, dark wood was a creepy, deserted cottage. Inside the cottage was a set of rickety, dusty stairs. At the top of the rickety, dusty stairs was a shadowy, cluttered attic. The attic hid an ancient secret.

Starting with some questions:

What was special about the attic? Why did I feel compelled to explore it that day last summer?

Starting with a conversation:

'W-w-what are you doing here?' I asked the ugly witch sitting on the end of my bed.
'I want it back!' she growled.
'W-w-what?' I stammered.
'You know what!' she snarled.

Starting by describing a character:

People say that I am small for my age. I have blond straight hair and some of my teeth have not grown in yet, so I have gaps in my mouth. My mum says that because I'm nosy I get into adventures.

THE MAGIC BOX – TEMPLATE

◆ Cut out and make up this magic box.
Then stick it to the back page of your book.

Back page of book

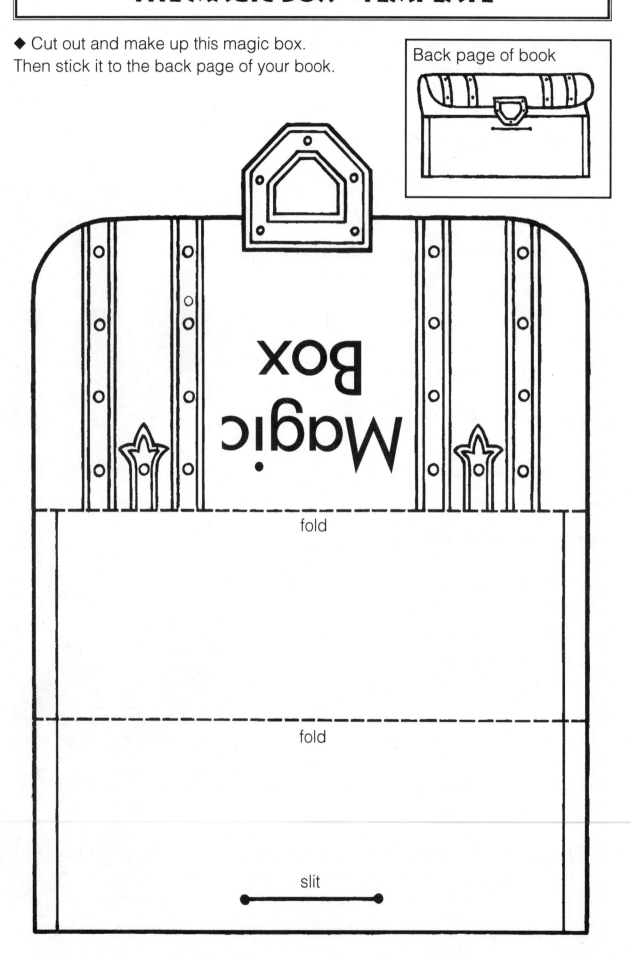

Magic
Box

fold

fold

slit

THE MAGIC BOX – EVALUATION

◆ When you read *The Magic Box*, think about the following questions:

1. Are the first sentences exciting?
2. Are the characters interesting?
3. Are there any good descriptions of places?
4. Does the story always make sense?
5. Is this a good story?
6. Are the illustrations well placed in the story?

Which aspect of the book is the most impressive? Explain why in the space below. Cut this out, fold it and place it in the box on the back cover of the book.

- ✂ - - -

The best thing about this story was:

Date: Signed:

- ✂ - - -

◆ When you read *The Magic Box*, think about the following questions:

1. Are the first sentences exciting?
2. Are the characters interesting?
3. Are there any good descriptions of places?
4. Does the story always make sense?
5. Is this a good story?
6. Are the illustrations well placed in the story?

Which aspect of the book is the most impressive? Explain why in the space below. Cut this out, fold it and place it in the box on the back cover of the book.

- ✂ - - -

The best thing about this story was:

Date: Signed:

THE MAGIC BOX – SELF-EVALUATION

◆ Read the story through from beginning to end and try to imagine what a friend who was reading it for the first time would think of your story. Now answer these questions:

Did you enjoy reading the story?

_____

Which parts do you think are particularly strong?

_____

_____

◆ Tick the words that apply particularly to this story and say why in the space below.

exciting	thrilling	mysterious	scary
well written	hard to follow	boring	funny
unclear	gripping	fast-moving	easy to read

Which part of the story do you think is best and why?

_____

_____

Are you pleased with the beginning? Why?

_____

_____

Is the storyline easy to follow? Is it too complicated? Is it too simple?

_____

_____

Scholastic
WRITING
Workshop

Chapter Four

ANIMAL
ADVENTURES

INTRODUCTION

Project description

In this project, the children work individually or in pairs to write a collection of short stories about an animal. They begin by inventing, with the help of photocopiable pages 39 and 40, a human personality for an animal or pet they know well. Alternatively they may like to invent an imaginary pet, if they don't have one of their own. Each child or pair then writes three to six short stories about events that happen to their animal. Each event is to be planned and written as a separate adventure with the central animal character as the one linking feature. Photocopiable sheets based on different possible story events support the children in generating ideas and structuring their stories.

It is best if all the children begin with the same story event to allow you to show them how best to use the photocopiable sheets. Thereafter, the children may select any story event and use the appropriate photocopiable page to support their ideas, or they may invent their own. Each story may be illustrated as it is drafted, or once the drafting and editing process has finished.

Why this context?

Children are familiar with, and love to read, animal stories. This project introduces children to the possibility of writing and sequencing a collection of short stories. The children have to think about how best to organise their collection and about the purpose and features of a good story title.

In requiring children to think about their pet or animal as a human, the project encourages them to invent rounded characters able to drive a story, to keep the characterisation consistent but also to develop it in the light of a variety of different experiences.

The photocopiable sheets support children by suggesting possible events that might spark a story. They help them both to think about a variety of possibilities within each story event and to use a device for ending stories that is common in children's books but rarely used when children write – rounding the story off by means of a conversation.

The celebration and evaluation process highlights some differences that may exist between readers, emphasising how personal preferences and experiences can produce different reader responses.

Project organisation

The project can be organised so that children work individually or in pairs. The whole class should begin by tackling the same story event so that you can explain the best way to use the photocopiable sheet as a springboard for ideas and for drafting parts of the story, as well as the issues to do with deciding on a title and ending the story with a conversation.

Paper, materials for illustrations and the photocopiable sheets supporting other story events must be prepared and available in advance because, after this, the children all work on their own choice of story events, either choosing to illustrate as they go or to do all the illustrations at the end. The photocopiable sheets offer such strong support that you may find that some short story events can be set as homework.

Ensure that the children know where to store finished stories and illustrations and where to put those on which they are still working.

At the start of the project set a clear deadline – perhaps two weeks hence – by which time each child should have produced 3–4 short stories and will be ready to design the cover, decide the sequence of stories and bind these into a book of short stories. The class can then work at the same time on the various publishing aspects.

Books the children may find useful

My Naughty Little Sister by Dorothy Edwards (Mammoth)
The Julian Stories by Ann Cameron (Victor Gollancz)
Milly-Molly-Mandy Stories by Joyce Lankester Brisley (Penguin)
A House Inside Out by Penelope Lively (Penguin)

Scholastic
IMAGINATIVE WRITING
Workshop

MEET MY PET

Teaching content
- Observation to build a description.
- Imparting human characteristics.

What you need
Photocopiable pages 39 and 40, accompanying audio cassette, a cassette player, writing materials.

What to do
This activity encourages children to use close observations in their writing and to develop and elaborate on these to build an imaginary personality that is larger than life.

Introduce this activity by playing the audio cassette interview with Dick King-Smith in which he talks about how he invents his animal characters. Why do the children think he prefers to create his characters from animals he knows well and has observed closely? How does this help him to develop personalities and ideas for storylines that are original and interesting?

Tell the children that they are going to write a series of short stories about an animal. Explain that they may choose any animal they like – their own pet, the pet of a neighbour or friend, a farm animal or a working animal, as long as

it is one that they know well and have been able to observe at close quarters. If the children are working in pairs, they need to choose one animal between them. If children can bring in a photograph of their animal, it would be valuable, but not absolutely necessary. Tell the children that each story will end with a short conversation between themselves and the animal, summing up the events of the story.

Give each child or pair copies of the photocopiable pages. Explain that photocopiable page 39 will help the children to focus their observations and descriptions of the animal. Photocopiable page 40 will help them to elaborate on their observations and build a human personality and voice for their chosen animal.

Suggest that the children complete as much of their photocopiable sheets in school as they can, but that they also take them home and add to them after more focused observation and, if possible, discussion with parents or friends who also know the animal well.

2

PLANNING, DRAFTING AND WRITING

✝/✝✝ ⏱60

Teaching content

Planning and carrying out a project consisting of different stories.

What you need

Photocopiable page 41 (if required), photocopiable pages 42–49 (ie. some for each story topic), writing materials, paper and art materials for illustrations.

What to do

This activity encompasses all the processes of planning, drafting and writing in one because its teaching objective is to provide children with the opportunity to plan for themselves how they tackle the whole task – whether they plan, draft and write each story in turn, or whether they plan them all first, then draft all, then write all – or a combination.

Explain that each child or pair is going to write a book containing three or four (maybe five or six per pair) short stories or adventures about their chosen animal. Each story will be about one event. The event can be true or imaginary. The important thing that the children should know is that, in all the stories, the animal can *speak*, although what it says can only be understood by the child writing the story (who is also a character in the story). This communication remains a secret between the child and the animal.

Explain that the children can base the stories on their own ideas, on things that have actually happened, or on the story ideas below, each of which is supported by a photocopiable sheet to help the children focus their ideas.

The day my animal...
• came to school
• made a friend
• got lost
• took a trip
• met a visitor
• saved the day
• made mum/dad mad
• became sick

Explain that several copies of each photocopiable sheet have been made, where they are stored and how children may get access to them. Emphasise to the children that they must read each photocopiable sheet through entirely before beginning to fill in responses. Responses should be written in brief note form of words and phrases.

Each story will end with the animal and child having a chat about the day's events before going to sleep and children should decide upon a final good night farewell that will end every story they write. Explain that it is this sort of convention that holds some books of short stories together when each adventure is new and different.

You may like to list all the topics on a poster somewhere in the classroom, or give each child a personal list to stick inside their drafting jotter, exercise book or writing folder and photocopiable page 41 is provided for this purpose. Explain that children should use these to keep a record of which stories they plan to write and their progress on each.

Most classes will benefit from being shown how to use the photocopiable sheets to generate ideas and structure the story. Selecting one initial story topic for all individuals in the class to work on allows the teacher to explain how to use the photocopiable sheets to elicit ideas and how to work from these to structure and write the story. A good starting point for such a class approach is 'The day my animal came to school', since the school is a context common to all.

The photocopiable pages have been designed to help children brainstorm ideas and draft parts of their stories. Key questions on each sheet invite different answers. Children should generate as many answers as possible and then select the best. Children must understand that the sole purpose of these sheets is to support them in thinking about the possibilities within a story. They do not have to base their story on the chosen sheet, or include all the ideas it mentions, if they would prefer not to do so. Each sheet ends in the same way and has been designed to support children in an aspect of storywriting that many find difficult – bringing the story to a satisfactory conclusion.

If the class is used to working independently and will be able to pace and organise their own work and to use the photocopiable sheets without much direct help, they could begin on any story idea that appeals to them.

Once children have decided their storylines and begun the first draft, provide unlined paper of various shapes and sizes for illustrations, along with suitable collage/art materials. Explain that children may choose to do illustrations as they draft their story, or wait until they are making the final copy at the end. If children choose to do the former, they must ensure that they do not end up with loads of illustrations but little writing. To help children in this respect, you may want to limit the number of illustrations per page, or per session.

Once each story has been written, children will need to choose a suitable title. This may be a topic for individual discussion with particular children. Alternatively, it can be made into a class teaching activity in several ways:

• Read one child's story to the whole class and ask everyone to write a title for it, then discuss which is best and why.
• Ask individual children to talk about their story and why they have chosen a particular title.
• Ask each child to generate two or three possible titles for one story and discuss with a friend which is best and why.

PUBLISHING THE BOOK
†/†† ○

Teaching content

Understanding how books of short stories are organised.

What you need

A selection of books of short stories (see list in introduction for suggestions), writing materials.

CELEBRATION AND EVALUATION

4

Teaching content

- Finding a reviewer.
- Compiling a set of reviews from different readers.

What you need

Completed 'Animal adventure' story collections, photocopiable page 50, writing materials.

What to do

Each short story collection needs to be read and reviewed by a selection of people. Encourage each child to identify the following types of people who might review their stories:
- an older child
- a parent
- a friend
- a teacher
- a neighbour

Give each reader a copy of photocopiable page 50 which will help to capture their personal reactions and opinions. The children should be encouraged to discuss the sheet with each reviewer and help them to complete it.

The completed sheets can be attached to the back of each book or displayed alongside it. Alternatively, the sheets from the whole class can be catalogued under the author's name and bound together in the form of a class reference book. When the short story books are displayed as general class reading, children should be encouraged to use the class catalogue to compare their own responses to the stories with those of others who have also read them.

What to do

Once the required number of short stories has been written, children must decide how to organise these into a volume of short stories.

Begin by asking the children to look at the books you have collected and to comment on how the reader knows which stories are in the book and how the stories are organised. Some books may have a short prologue introducing the main character in question, others will simply launch into the first story and rely on this to introduce the character. Most of the books will have a contents page with the stories listed in sequence, and sometimes the page number. Some books may have a separate title page and illustration before each story; others will simply have the story title at the top of the page.

Tell the children to decide how they would like to organise their stories into a book and to make appropriate provision to indicate this for the reader. They should decide on an overall title for the book, and make a front cover and title page. On the back cover, they may wish to write a short piece about the author or a publisher's blurb about the stories in the book. There are specific activities in the chapter on presentation which cover these tasks.

MEET MY PET

Type of animal _____   Name of animal _____

Age of animal _____   Owner of animal _____

Describe your animal. How would you recognise it from any other of its type?

_____

_____

_____

Describe your animal sleeping. What does it do with its legs? its head?
its tail? its ears? Where does it like to sleep?

_____

_____

_____

How does your animal show that it is hungry? What does it do
when food arrives?

_____

_____

_____

What (or who) makes your animal cross? What does it do?

_____

_____

_____

What games does your animal like to play? What does it do when
it wants to play?

_____

_____

_____

MEET MY PET

◆ If your animal could speak, what would it be like? Circle the best words and add any others that decribe your animal.

old, young, bossy, careful, fussy, carefree, messy, tidy, reckless, optimistic, proud, deceitful, nervous, timid, wily, sly, friendly, lazy, stupid, jealous, laid-back, organised, hard-working, quick, perfectionist, leader, noisy, follower, loner, gang member, funny, cheerful, miserable, sleepy, greedy.

What sort of voice would your animal have? Would it have an accent?

_____

What would it say about:
• you and other members of your family? _____

_____

• other animals in the neighbourhood? _____

_____

• what it likes to do with you? _____

_____

• bathtime? _____

• bedtime? _____

• feeding time? _____

• the food it likes/dislikes? _____

_____

• its favourite room/place? _____

_____

PLANNING, DRAFTING AND WRITING

IP = ideas planned
D = story in draft form
E = story edited – ready for good copy
FC = story copied and illustrated

The day my animal:

came to school

made a friend

got lost

took a trip

met a visitor

saved the day

made mum/dad mad

became sick

IP = ideas planned
D = story in draft form
E = story edited – ready for good copy
FC = story copied and illustrated

The day my animal:

came to school

made a friend

got lost

took a trip

met a visitor

saved the day

made mum/dad mad

became sick

IP = ideas planned
D = story in draft form
E = story edited – ready for good copy
FC = story copied and illustrated

The day my animal:

came to school

made a friend

got lost

took a trip

met a visitor

saved the day

made mum/dad mad

became sick

IP = ideas planned
D = story in draft form
E = story edited – ready for good copy
FC = story copied and illustrated

The day my animal:

came to school

made a friend

got lost

took a trip

met a visitor

saved the day

made mum/dad mad

became sick

THE DAY MY ANIMAL CAME TO SCHOOL

◆ Read the whole page before you begin.

How did it get to school?

_____

_____

_____

Who saw it first? What did they say? What did they do?

_____

_____

_____

What did it do to make its presence known?

_____

_____

_____

How did it cause chaos?

_____

_____

_____

What did people say?

the headteacher _____

the class teacher _____

the secretary _____

other children _____

What did it say about...?

_____

_____

_____

_____

What happened in the end?

◆ On the other side of this page, write what you and your animal said to each other about the adventure at the end of the day.

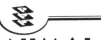

THE DAY MY CROSS ANIMAL MADE A FRIEND

◆ Read the whole page before you begin.

Why was it in a bad mood?

_____

_____

_____

How did it show it was cross?

_____

_____

_____

Who did it meet – human or animal?

_____

_____

_____

What was their first reaction?

_____

_____

_____

The friend did something that made your animal laugh. What was it?

_____

_____

What did these characters say to themselves?   What did they say out loud?

Your animal _____   _____

The friend _____   _____

You _____   _____

What happened in the end?

◆ On the other side of this page, write what you and your animal said to each other about the adventure at the end of the day.

THE DAY MY ANIMAL GOT LOST

◆ Read the whole page before you begin.
You and your animal went visiting to a certain place for the first time.

Where was this place and why were you visiting?

_____

_____

Somehow, you and your animal became separated. How did this happen?

_____

_____

When did you discover that your animal was lost?   What did you say or shout?

_____

_____

◆ Here is a list of ways in which you may have found your animal. Either tick the one you will use in your story or write an idea of your own.

• You rang the police and found out that someone had taken your animal to the police station. ☐

• You spent hours walking and calling in all directions and your animal finally heard you. ☐

• Your animal found its own way home and you found it there when you returned in despair! ☐

• Your animal was trapped (or perhaps stolen) and, as you searched, you heard it calling. ☐

• Another idea... ☐

What did you say when you met?

_____

_____

What sort of celebration did you have?

_____

_____

◆ On the other side of this page, write what you and your animal said to each other about the adventure at the end of the day.

THE DAY MY ANIMAL TOOK A TRIP

◆ Read the whole page before you begin.
You and your animal had to take a trip to a place it had never seen before.

Where was the place?

☐ seaside   ☐ mountains

☐ countryside ☐ busy city

☐ other _____

Describe it in a list of ideas:

sounds _____

sights _____

colours _____

smells _____

How did you travel?

_____

_____

How did you feel about the place?

_____

_____

How did you show your feelings?

_____

_____

How did your animal feel about the place?

_____

_____

How did it show its feelings?

_____

_____

What did you do in this place?

_____

_____

How long did you stay?

_____

_____

What did you say as you left?

_____

_____

Will you ever return?

_____

_____

What did your animal say as it left?

_____

_____

How did you both feel about returning home?

_____

_____

◆ On the other side of this page, write what you and your animal said to each other about the adventure at the end of the day.

THE DAY MY ANIMAL MET A VISITOR

◆ Read the whole page before you begin.
Animals are very good at sensing whether people can be trusted or not.
A visitor came to your house.

Who was it?

_____

_____

Your animal didn't like/trust the visitor. How did it show its feelings?

tail:

eyes:

movements:

sounds:

Your family was embarrassed by this behaviour. What did they say?

_____

_____

What did you say?

_____

_____

What did the visitor say?

_____

_____

You left your house suddenly and found the visitor outside doing something bad to your animal. What was it?

Who did you tell about the visitor?

_____

_____

_____

_____

What happened in the end?

◆ On the other side of this page, write what you and your animal said to each other about the adventure at the end of the day.

THE DAY MY ANIMAL SAVED THE DAY

◆ Read the whole page before you begin.
Tick the event that caused your animal to save the day.

A house fire ☐

A gang of bullies attacked you ☐

You fell over a cliff and were left hanging by your fingertips ☐

A burglar broke in ☐

Someone alone in your house fell downstairs and was unable to get help ☐

Another idea... ☐

Write the headline in the local paper about the event.

_____

_____

_____

When interviewed about the event, what did you say to the newspaper reporter about your animal?

_____

_____

_____

What did your mum or dad say?

_____

_____

_____

Did your animal fetch help or deal with the situation itself? How?

_____

_____

_____

How was your animal rewarded?

_____

_____

_____

◆ On the other side of this page, write what you and your animal said to each other about the adventure at the end of the day.

THE DAY MY ANIMAL MADE MUM/DAD MAD

◆ Read the whole page before you begin.

There is something that your mum or dad will not allow your animal to do.

What is it?

_____

_____

_____

What did you say?

_____

_____

_____

Behind their backs you sometimes allowed your animal to do this thing. At what time might this happen?

_____

_____

_____

What did your mum or dad say and do?

_____

_____

_____

How did your mum or dad find your animal doing this thing?

_____

_____

_____

How did your animal show that it was sorry?

_____

_____

_____

What happened in the end?

◆ On the other side of this page, write what you and your animal said to each other about the adventure at the end of the day.

THE DAY MY ANIMAL BECAME SICK

◆ Read the whole page before you begin.

What illness did your animal have?

_____

_____

How did it show that it was ill?

_____

_____

Where did you take your animal to find out what was wrong?

_____

_____

How did you get there?

_____

_____

How did you comfort your animal on the journey?

_____

_____

What did the medicine look like that was given for the illness?

_____

_____

What did the label say?

[ ]

Your animal hated the medicine. How did you make it swallow this?

_____

_____

What did you and your animal do during the night?

_____

_____

What worries did you have?

_____

_____

How did you know your animal was feeling better?.

_____

_____

◆ On the other side of this page, write what you and your animal said to each other about the adventure at the end of the day.

ANIMAL ADVENTURES – EVALUATION

◆ Please answer the following questions in as much detail as possible:

1. Did you like the central animal character? What did you like best about him/her? Why?

_____

_____

_____

2. Which of the stories did you like best? Why?

_____

_____

3. Look at the story titles. Which did you think was most effective? Why?

_____

_____

4. Think about how each story ended. Which ending did you like best? Why?

_____

_____

_____

5. In your opinion, was this the best sequence for the stories or would you have put them in a different order? How would you have ordered the stories and why?

_____

_____

_____

6. Comment on the cover, the title of the collection, the illustrations and general presentation.

_____

_____

7. Would you like to read another short story collection about this animal?

_____

_____

8. Would you like to read another short story collection by this author?

_____

_____

Scholastic WRITING Workshop

Chapter Five

TOP DOG AT LAST

INTRODUCTION

Project description

This is a short and highly structured context in which young or inexperienced writers are strongly supported in writing a 'Happy ending' story. The context begins with class discussion and analysis of story plots in which everyone lives happily ever after. A happy ending generally follows a very sad beginning. Children are told that they are to write such a story about a sad, neglected dog. In groups of four they brainstorm vocabulary to describe this animal in general terms. A more particular description is written individually after children research breeds of dog and choose one to be the hero of their story. These descriptions are evaluated by writing partners.

The children next decide the cause of the dog's sad state and then write the story, using a starter sentence if they need this support. In the third part of the story, children describe themselves finding and caring for the dog and the end tells of the two new friends enjoying each other's company and, of course, living happily ever after!

Why this context?

Motivation is very important for young writers and in this context there are two ingredients that children love to write about. One is an animal and the other is a happy ending. The project demands that writers describe an animal and they are helped in this by brainstorming in groups and then by researching a particular breed of dog. Each part of the story is short and created through a structured activity. Starter sentences are provided to help the story to flow smoothly. The almost certain success of the project gives writers an immense sense of achievement.

Project organisation

The children should be given a storage envelope, a tray or filing space in which to organise ongoing writing.

The children first discuss story structure as a class and then brainstorm vocabulary in groups of four. They research and individually choose a breed of dog about which to write. Initial descriptions are shared with writing partners who are asked to comment and, after thinking time, children tell their sad stories to the same partners.

Finally, writers individually complete rough drafts and then possibly re-write and illustrate their stories in an interesting publishing format.

Children store the individual story parts as the writing progresses. When they have completed the storyline, decisions will be made as to which parts need re-writing, some children possibly choosing to re-write on the word processor.

Publication and presentation

Story parts may be written on lined paper and illustrations drawn on pieces of unlined, possibly coloured paper Stories may be stuck on to larger sheets of sugar paper to provide borders, and stapled or sewn into a book format. Alternatively, a large dog shape may be cut from card or sugar paper and the story may be stuck on to this, together with the illustrations.

Children are encouraged to hold a story-reading session at home.

Books the children may find useful

Frankie Makes a Friend by Tony Bradman (Andersen Press)
No Roses for Harry by Gene Zion and Margaret Bloy Graham (Penguin)
Fair's Fair by Leon Garfield (Simon & Schuster)
Underdog by Marilyn Sachs (Oxford University Press)
The Guard Dog by Dick King-Smith (Doubleday)

1

A SAD BEGINNING

Teaching content

- Building vocabulary for a description.
- Focusing on genre of happy-ending stories.

What you need

Photocopiable page 57 (blown up to A3 size if possible).

What to do

Explain to the children that they will be writing a 'happy-ending story' about a dog. Discuss with them the idea that a happy ending implies that something sad must have happened at the beginning of the story. Ask them to give examples of happy-ending animal stories they know and write these on the board. How do these stories begin? (If the children have already read *The Guard Dog* by Dick King-Smith, use this as an example.) Discuss the different sorts of sad beginnings their story about a dog could have. If children need prompting, suggest some of the following ideas:

- A dog is given as a Christmas or birthday present but is soon left forgotten or unwanted.
- A dog's beloved owner dies, leaving him alone.
- A dog is kept prisoner by cruel owners.
- A dog is attacked by other dogs or animals.

Arrange the children in groups of four and give each group a copy of photocopiable page 57. Ask them to brainstorm vocabulary and phrases to describe a dog in an unhappy or neglected condition. They should write these in under the main features labelled, adding any other features they wish. An example is shown in the illustration. After 5–10 minutes, ask the children to report back on what they have written. Display these brainstorms on the wall.

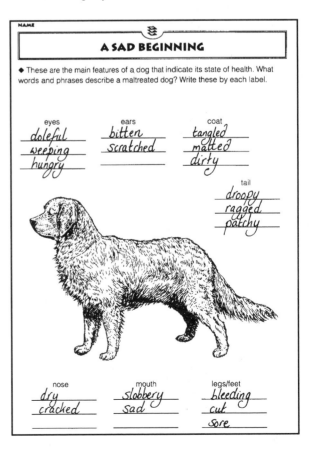

2

A TEAR TO THE EYE

Teaching content
Writing emotive descriptions.

What you need
Access to brainstorm ideas from previous session, reference books about dogs, writing and drawing materials.

What to do
Tell the children they need to decide what sort of dog they will write about. It may be a particular breed or a mongrel. Allow children time to consult reference books and decide upon a dog that they really like and would love to own.

Now ask the children to sketch the dog they have chosen, copying from books or inventing a mongrel. When they have completed their sketch, ask them to write a description of their dog when it is in a very sorry state. Encourage the writers to use ideas from the brainstorms displayed on the wall. Stress that this writing is a description of what the dog looks like and should not mention how the dog came to be in this state.

Ask the children to swap completed descriptions with a writing partner, and explain that if the description has been well written, it should bring a tear to the eye of the reader. Let them make any adjustments they wish, following

their partner's response. Once finished, tell the children to keep these drafts in a safe place.

Ask the children to decide overnight what has happened to leave their dog in this miserable state. They should come to school tomorrow having made a firm decision about this.

3

THE DOG'S STORY

Teaching content
Telling a coherent tale.

What you need
Writing materials.

What to do
Ask the children to tell their writing partners what has happened to cause their dog such misery. This will help to form the story and partners may ask questions if there are inconsistencies or gaps in the narrative.

Write the following sentence on the board: 'Whining softly and limping sadly, the wretched animal remembered what had happened...' The children should use this as the first sentence and then, individually, write the story that they have just told their writing partner. Tell the children to keep this rough draft in a safe place along with their dog descriptions.

4

TURNING POINT: CHILD MEETS DOG

Teaching content
• Writing about self in third person.
• Writing a turning point.

What you need
Writing materials.

What to do
Explain to the children that they now have a description of their dog and a description of what has happened to the dog in the past. Now

tell the children that as the dog limps sadly along, thinking of its past, it turns into their (the child's) very own road and collapses, exhausted, beside their front door.

Ask the children to imagine what happens when they discover the dog. Do they discover it alone, with a friend or with a parent or other family member? Get them to write what they say and what they do, but explain that this must not be written in the first person; the whole story has been told from the viewpoint of a narrator and so this and the final part in the next activity must also be told from this perspective.

If children wish they can share their writing with a writing partner and amend if necessary. Tell them then to put this rough draft with the others in a safe place.

5

A HAPPY ENDING

Teaching content
Writing a happy ending.

What you need
Writing materials.

What to do
Explain to the children that they must now conclude their story with a happy ending. Remind them that a satisfying ending requires that all problems are resolved, so they must refer back to what they have already written and make sure that their ending answers all questions – for example, if their dog was injured, how does it recover?

Suggest that the children might end the story with a description of the child and the dog doing something enjoyable together. What is the dog like now that it has been nursed back to health by its new owner? How do the dog and owner behave towards each other?

Let the children share their writing with their writing partner, asking the critical question: is the ending good? Does it answer all the reader's questions?

6

PRESENTING THE STORY

Teaching content
Focusing on authorship, presentation and audience.

What you need
Four drafts from activities 2–5, writing and book-making materials.

What to do
Tell the children that they are now ready to make their story into a book and that they can choose how to do this. Explain that often the way stories are presented depends on who is going to read them. For example, if the story is meant for very young children, it might be

presented as a shape book – that is with all the pages cut into the shape of a dog, or a dog's head – or as a zigzag book. If the story is for an older reader, it might be presented as a conventional paperback – perhaps like *The Guard Dog* with black line drawings, or like *The Man Whose Mother Was a Pirate* with colour illustrations, or like *Fair's Fair* and *Matthew and the Sea Singer* with both!

So, first the children must decide on the most appropriate format for their main audience. Give them a variety of shapes and sizes of plain paper for illustrations, and lined paper for copying out the story. Explain that they can organise the time allotted as they wish, deciding when to copy out the storyline and when to work on their illustrations. Remind them that illustrations can be any shape and size and placed anywhere on the page. Give them a fixed time for this task.

Once finished, tell the children to mount their writing on to pre-cut pages and staple or bind them together to make a book. To complete the project, they should design a front cover and title page, and write a passage 'About the author' for the back cover of the book. If the children need guidance there are specific activities covering these tasks in the chapter on presentation.

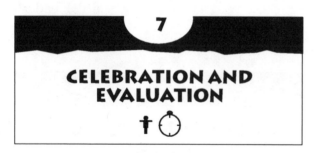

7

CELEBRATION AND EVALUATION

† ◯

Teaching content
Writers tell their stories.

What you need
Completed 'Top dog at last' books, an audience at school or at home, photocopiable page 58, writing materials, candles (optional), camera (optional).

What to do
'Top dog at last' is the sort of weepy, happy-ending story that everyone enjoys. The story is also short enough to engage close attention from readers and listeners alike. Depending upon the type of school, children and parents, this could be an opportunity for writers to take their stories home to hold a story-reading

session. If this activity is inappropriate for your school, arrange for small groups of children from other classes to come and listen to the stories.

Explain to the children that they are going to provide entertainment for their families or for a group of friends by reading their stories. They must create quiet, comfortable conditions to ensure that the audience settles and listens carefully. Perhaps they could provide drinks for the listeners. If adults are present, then lighting a few candles can create a peaceful listening ambience. Warn children that candles must never be lit for a purely children's audience. When the story is finished then the audience should be invited to fill in the evaluation form on photocopiable page 58.

When practising for the story-reading, there are activities in the presentation chapter that may help with preparation.

Some parents may be willing to photograph the story-telling session. If your school has a camera, you may be able to arrange for the children to borrow it for an evening each so that every child has a photograph of their story-telling session. Photographs and evaluation forms may be displayed with the books in the classroom.

A SAD BEGINNING

◆ These are the main features of a dog that indicate its state of health. What words and phrases describe a maltreated dog? Write these by each label.

eyes   ears   coat

_____   _____   _____

_____   _____   _____

_____   _____   _____

                                                tail

                                                _____

                                                _____

                                                _____

nose   mouth   legs/feet

_____   _____   _____

_____   _____   _____

_____   _____   _____

TOP DOG AT LAST – EVALUATION

◆ Before the days of television or radio, during the dark winter months, people used to enjoy listening to a good story-teller reading or telling stories.

Today you will hear a story and after this would you please answer the following questions about this event:

• Did the story-teller make you feel comfortable before beginning?

Comment:

• Did the story-teller read in a clear voice and at a good pace?

Comment:

• Did you want to cry at the beginning of the story? Why?

Comment:

• Did you like the dog in this story? Why?

Comment:

• What did you think of the end of the story?

Comment:

• Would you like to read or hear more stories from this story-teller?

Comment:

Chapter Six

THE MONSTERS' FEAST

INTRODUCTION

Project description

In this project children write a story which has a frightening, mysterious opening but ends in high farce. The basic events of the story are pre-determined and map on to sections of a silhouette zigzag book. Through inventing the characters and fleshing out the details, the children make their story their own and different from any other.

They begin by imagining that one dark night a mysterious monster arrives in their town. They invent their monster and write a scary story opener which describes it walking down the street towards their school. A drama lesson helps the children to decide what happens inside the school when their monster joins other visiting monsters for an outrageous party. Finally they all depart, leaving a terrible mess. The next morning the headteacher discovers the debris and writes a serious letter of complaint. The story ends with an envelope containing this letter.

Why this context?

Children's literature, films and television abound with stories of monsters, giving those children who are not avid readers a rich and diverse bank of ideas on which to draw. Children relish the opportunity to invent their own monster and willingly mix their own ideas with those drawn from other sources.

As in the best monster stories, this project mixes horror with humour and fantasy with fact. The basic story outline is provided, leaving children to invent their own details within a fairly tight structure.

The story is set in the children's own environment, which offers support in thinking about the details of place while challenging writers to select and describe specific features to create different effects. For example, children have to describe a familiar street in a way that creates an atmosphere of tension and foreboding, but use their description of a place in the school to prepare the reader for a much happier scene.

In this project children embellish their personal experience of events and places to portray a fantasy monster world. They learn how to incorporate different forms of writing into an imaginative story, inventing and writing dialogue, menus and formal letters and they are shown how these may be used to move the story forward.

Project organisation

The project starts with individual work as children make a monster, write a short character background and an atmospheric description of the journey of this monster to the school. In groups of three, children invent and describe how their monsters meet and the events of the monsters' feast. Each child then works, with support from a photocopiable sheet, to write and produce the story as an individual publication.

Because the overall organisation and structure of this project offers such strong support, the majority of writers will be able to forge ahead on each task, allowing you time to observe the children as they work and to target particular individuals for attention. This is easiest to manage if the class is generally kept 'together', with you ensuring that all the children have completed each stage before the next task is introduced.

Publication and presentation

The story is presented as a silhouette zigzag book, with each section describing a discrete part of the story. An envelope containing the headteacher's letter is stuck on to one of the final sections of the story, along with evidence of the night's happenings.

Two levels of evaluation sheets, suitable for children from younger or older classes are provided. These can be completed when the children share their 'Monsters' Feast' stories with their friends or if the books are read by children in another class in the school. Positive comments can be cut from these and stuck on to the final page of the book to provide short reviews for other readers.

Books the children may find useful

Where the Wild Things Are by Maurice Sendak (Penguin)
Library Monster by Anne Forsyth (Hamish Hamilton)
Monster Monday by Anne Forsyth (Hamish Hamilton)
Monica's Monster by Sheila Lavelle (Hodder)
Have You Seen Who's Just Moved in Next Door to Us? by Colin McNaughton (Walker Books)
Monster Birthday Party by Carolyn Dinan (Hamish Hamilton)

INVENTING THE MONSTER
✝ 60

Teaching content
Creating a character with a background.

What you need
Either prepared zigzag books or paper to make them, pencils, felt-tipped pens, scissors, chalkboard.

What to do
Explain to the children that they are going to invent a monster from outer space that lands somewhere near to their school. The monster's adventure will unfold slowly, but the first thing the children must do is make their own monster.

Give each child a zigzag book or show them how to make one by folding a length of paper into a zigzag. Explain that the first page will be the front cover of a book with a picture of the main character in the story as well as the title of the book, 'The Monsters' Feast', and the name of the author. Tell them to draw a box at the bottom of the page for the title and the name of the author. Now ask the children to imagine what their monster will look like and to draw a picture of it so that it fills up the rest of the space on the page, actually touching the top edge of the paper.

When they have finished drawing the monster, the children should colour it in with felt-tipped pens and cut around the very top part of the shape, thus producing the front cover of a silhouette book, as shown. Make sure they only cut through one page, as subsequent pages will have different silhouettes.

As the children complete this task, ask them to think of answers to the following questions, which should be written on the board:
• What is the monster's name?
• Where does the monster come from?
• Why has the monster come to Earth?
This information should be written in the centre of the next page.

THE COMING OF THE MONSTER
Ⓦ→ⱦⱦⱦ→✝ 60

Teaching content
• Setting the scene.
• Creating an atmosphere of fear and suspense.

What you need
Large sheets of paper, marker pens, paper, writing and drawing materials, zigzag books, glue, scissors.

What to do
Explain to the children that they are now going to write the first part of the story. This will tell how the monster, having landed in the local area, makes its way towards the children's school, finds the school building and seeks shelter there. The atmosphere that needs to be generated in this section of writing is one of fear and suspense. suggest that the children look at pages 6–7 from *A Lion at Bedtime* by Debi Gliori as an example of this.

Having outlined the direction in which the story will be moving, discuss with the children the way in which film and novel writers often

ABOUT THE MONSTER

Dennis is my monsters name. He comes from the barn up in the mountain. My monster favourite food is stones. His worst enemy is Dragon hunter.

His height is the same as mine. His age as 8. He doesnt have a family. He lives on a hill.

CHAPTER ONE
The Coming

It was a very dark night in Fintry and there was a flash of thunder. Then suddenly there were foot steps being heard. He was wandering in the night. Somebody saw his tail and started to follow him but the

create this kind of atmosphere by setting the scene at particular times of day and in certain weather conditions. For instance, a scene in the night-time fog would appear much more mysterious and threatening than the same scene in the midday sun.

Organise the children into groups of three. These groups will be working together on this writing project through several important activities and so must be chosen carefully. Give each group a poster-sized sheet of paper and a marker pen and ask them to brainstorm on the sheet all the words and phrases they can think of to create an atmosphere of tension and fear. After 5–10 minutes a spokesperson for each group should report back, then the brainstorm posters can be displayed, thus building up a bank of vocabulary for the class.

Using the group brainstorm and other ideas collected from the class discussion, the children should now work individually to write a paragraph describing the monster's journey from its landing place to the school.

When they have edited and re-drafted their writing to produce a version they are happy with, the children should draw a sketch of the school on the third page of their zigzag books. The sketch should touch the top of the page and take up about a quarter of the page in depth. When the sketches are finished the children should cut around the top shape, creating a rooftop silhouette. Under this they should write the first chapter number and

heading, and copy or stick in their Chapter One. This may extend over to page 4 of the book or this page may be used for illustration.

3

THE MEETING
ᵗᵗᵗ–ⓦ ⑥⁰

Teaching content
- Using drama to help invent dialogue.
- Learning to criticise a play in a positive and helpful way.

What you need
Photocopiable page 68, writing materials.

What to do
Explain to the children that, having arrived at the school and believing it is alone, their monster is surprised to discover that there are other monsters in the building. Tell the children that, in their groups of three, they are going to make up and perform mini-dramas of the monsters' initial meeting. Each child will play the part of his or her monster and they will meet up with each other. What will they say to one another? What questions will they ask? Allow the groups 5–10 minutes to practise, then get a few groups to perform their dramas to the rest

of the class. Ask for positive comments on each performance and then ask for advice about improvements that could be made.

Use this feedback session as a means of guiding the direction that dramas may take. Children will often use drama as an expression for aggression and anger. Encourage the development of friendly, curious meetings rather than frightening, aggressive approaches.

Now give the children a further 5–10 minutes to make any necessary changes to their plays and tell them that at the end of that time all the groups will perform, giving their plays a title and finding a way to show that the performance has reached an end. A bow and a cheery wave from the performers may indicate this.

It is important for the teacher to create a sense of speed and energy in this session. Without speed, not all plays will be seen and children work with greater focus if they are given time limits. These may always be expanded by adding an extra few minutes if necessary. Every performance should be applauded at the end and two or three positive comments should be invited from the audience for each play.

Finally, in their groups ask the children to fill in the theatre critic's report on photocopiable page 68. It is a good idea to allocate a play to each group because, if left to free choice, all will tend to want to comment on the best production and it is important that all groups receive feedback. Stress that comments are intended to be helpful and so must be positive.

4

WRITING ABOUT THE MEETING

Teaching content
Writing dialogue.

What you need
Selection of novels, photocopiable page 69, writing and drawing materials, zigzag books, scissors, glue.

What to do
Explain that each group is now going to write up the next part of the story which is about the meeting of the three monsters. Children will be able to use their plays as a basis for this, but point out how confusing it would be for the reader if this were written merely as a list of what characters said to each other. Ask the children to find one page containing a lot of dialogue from any novel in the class library. Discuss how to recognise a page of dialogue when flicking through a book. This will introduce or remind children about the conventions of speech marks. Ask the groups to study their particular page of dialogue and pick out examples of how the writer indicates who is speaking.

When watching a play it is obvious who is speaking and the tone and delivery of every statement is made clear by the actor. In a book it is the job of the writer to show all of these things. Ask for examples of how writers indicate mood and tone of delivery and also the movement or position of the speaker within a scene. Writers usually have to state this explicitly. Give each child a copy of photocopiable page 69 which contains a piece of dialogue written firstly as a drama script and then included in a passage of narrative. This should help them to see the difference in form quite clearly.

While looking at the narrative passage, point out that whenever a new person speaks, the writer begins a new paragraph. Writers do this because writing direct speech or dialogue into a story can become very confusing with all the necessary punctuation. If each new speaker begins talking on a new line, this helps to clarify speech and action.

Explain to the children how important it is not to keep repeating the word 'said' after each character speaks but to enrich the expression of the writing by using instead a word that says *how* the speaker delivered his statement. Give

a few verbal examples and then ask for further oral examples of this, for example:
- 'Don't go!' Mary wept.
- 'Don't go!' Peter commanded.
- 'Don't go!' pleaded the child.
- Don't go!' shouted the crossing attendant.

In their groups, the children should now write up a rough draft describing the monsters' meeting. This is a difficult writing task and the support of three writers will prove very helpful. The rough draft should then be edited, re-drafted and given a chapter heading to produce a final draft, which may be photocopied so that all three children have a copy of the next part of their story. A further copy of each group's final draft should also be displayed alongside the theatre critic's reports. As all the children will be familiar with the dramas presented to the class they should find it interesting to compare final write-ups.

The silhouette for Chapter Two of the story is an arc, representing the ceiling of the room in which the meeting takes place. Lights should be drawn hanging from this and then the rest of the room completed. Chapter Two should be stuck under this. This part of the story may go on to page 6 or that page may be used for illustration.

THE MONSTERS' FEAST

Teaching content
Imaginative ideas written up in functional style in order to carry plot forward and help to create context.

What you need
Paper, writing materials, pieces of card (approximately 8 x 13cm), art materials.

What to do
Explain that when they realise that there are many more monsters visiting the school on this strange weekend, the monsters decide to have a feast and invite all the others. In their groups of three the children must decide:
- what food to have on the menu;
- what party games will be played;
- where in the school the party will be held;
- which day and at what time it will take place.

The children will enjoy deciding these points and you may want to set ground rules for dishes on the menu as these will probably become extremely disgusting if you allow the groups a completely free rein. Explain that writers often want to amuse or even shock readers to some extent but they don't want to make them sick!

A great deal of fun can be had from playing on the words of well-known games and foods. Children are remarkably clever with puns when given the opportunity in activities like this.

Having answered the above questions in rough, the groups should then decide which person is to make the final copy of:
1. the monster feast menu;
2. the list of party games;
3. an invitation to the feast.
These items should be produced on card, decorated, and kept by the child for use at the end of the writing project.

6

THE STORY OF THE FEAST

Teaching content
Combining individual contributions, ensuring consistency.

What you need
Photocopiable page 70, scissors, writing materials, zigzag books, glue.

What to do
In their groups of three, the children will now write the story of the monsters' feast which constitutes Chapter Three of the book. Explain that it will be told from the point of view of an objective narrator but each child will take responsibility for writing up one paragraph of the story.

The planning for the three paragraphs should be done by all three children together so that everyone has a clear perception of the atmosphere and the events that take place at the feast. They should work out a clear line of progression and decide on the endings of the paragraphs so that they follow on neatly from each other.

Photocopiable page 70 will provide a framework for brainstorming and organising ideas. The three sections may be cut out and handed to the children responsible for particular paragraphs.

When the children have each produced a rough copy of their paragraphs, tell them to re-read all three paragraphs carefully to iron out any discrepancies and ensure the flow of the story is smooth at 'joins' between writers.

The whole final version should be re-written neatly by all three children so that they each have a copy for their individual books. If time is short, then children may re-write their own parts and these could be pasted together and photocopied so that every child gets a copy. Of course, this is the perfect opportunity to use a word processor in the interests of uniformity.

Decide whether to use the paragraph headings on the photocopiable page or to leave them out so that the story reads in one continuous flow.

The silhouette for the top of page 7 is one of party balloons, which the children should draw touching the top of the page and then cut around carefully. They should then write the chapter number and heading 'Monster Feast' and stick in their chapter. This will probably be quite long and can extend to page 11 if necessary.

HEADTEACHER IN A RAGE

ⓦ-✝ ⑥⓪

Teaching content
Writing an epilogue.

What you need
Matthew and the Sea Singer, writing materials, zigzag books, glue, envelopes, sheet of the headteacher's official writing paper; menus, lists of party games and invitations from activity 5 'The Monsters' Feast'.

What to do
The children may have come across an example of an epilogue in their reading. Try to elicit from their own reading experience what use an epilogue has in a story. It is a brief afterword, sometimes explaining what happened to characters as a result of the happenings in the book. Show them the last page of *Matthew and the Sea Singer* and explain that this forms an epilogue to the story. Tell the children that they are going to write an epilogue to describe what happened in the school as a result of the monsters' feast.

To set the scene, explain to them that the day after the feast, the headteacher arrives in school to find a certain part of the building in chaos. The headteacher decides to write to someone in highest authority to complain about what has happened to the school and to demand immediate action.

The headteacher's letter is the epilogue to the story and will be included in an envelope stuck in to the book. Readers can open the envelope to read the epilogue. The headteacher also sends one piece of evidence with her letter – either the list of party games, the invitation or the menu made in activity 5. Each child should still have the piece of evidence that was produced in that activity. This will also be stuck in to the book under the heading 'Evidence'.

The children should write the headteacher's letter individually. Firstly, they should brainstorm as a class the people to whom she might write to complain about the chaos in the school and to ask that the intruders be found and punished.

The brainstorm will probably produce such wide-ranging ideas as: the Director of Education, the police, a local M.P., the Prime Minister or even the Queen.

It is interesting next to look at conventions used for writing official letters. New technology has led to changes in the way letters are set out and it may be useful to check school policy on this or ask the school secretary how official letters are written in your school. If possible, show the children some examples.

Discuss the kind of language people use when writing angry, complaining letters and brainstorm some common phrases, for example:

- 'I am writing to complain about...'
- 'I am shocked to discover...'

Now ask the children to compose a letter in which the headteacher explains what she discovered upon going into school on the fateful morning after the monsters' feast. The letter should refer to the piece of evidence found at the scene. Next she should ask for help to deal with the matter and then sign off with a final phrase or sentence such as:

- 'I hope that you can attend to this matter soon.'
- 'Hoping to hear from you soon about this matter.'

Explain that official letters are signed 'Yours faithfully' if you don't know the name of the person you're writing to, and 'Yours sincerely' if you do.

It adds to the fun and authenticity of this letter if the final draft is written on a photocopy of the headteacher's official notepaper.

The envelope for the headteacher's letter should be stuck on to the next available page. The page after this should be headed 'Evidence' and the menu, the invitation or the list of party games should be stuck underneath. Finally, the remaining blank pages of the zigzag book could be filled with ideas from the chapter on presentation. Children may like to create an 'About the author' page, a publisher's blurb or some critics' reviews.

8

CELEBRATION AND REVIEW

Teaching content
Readers enjoy stories for different reasons.

What you need
Monsters' Feast zigzag books, photocopiable pages 71 and 72, writing materials.

What to do
When all the Monsters' Feast story books have been completed, arrange for the children to read them to individuals in another class in the school. If the children have not done this before, it may be necessary to talk about how to do this and give them an opportunity to practise reading the story aloud. Use activity 16 'Practising reading aloud' from the presentation chapter to do this if you wish. In particular remind the children of the importance of showing younger children the illustrations as the story unfolds and involving them in the story experience.

After the reading session, negotiate some time in which the child who has listened to the story can complete an evaluation sheet, assisted by the author. A younger class should use evaluation sheet B on photocopiable page 72 and an older class or peer group should use sheet A on photocopiable page 71.

Older children may want a younger author to clarify problems with handwriting and they should be prepared to show enjoyment while reading, exclaiming over good points and beautiful presentation. Make sure the listeners understand the value of positive feedback.

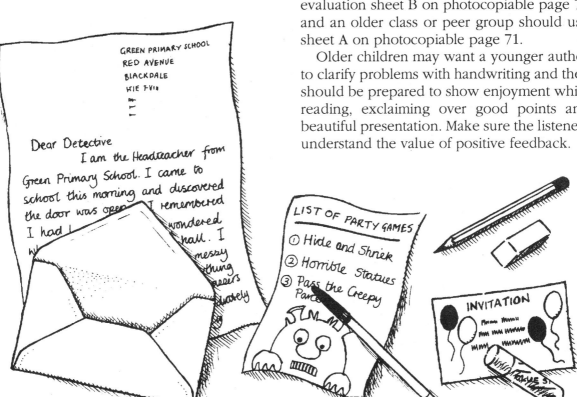

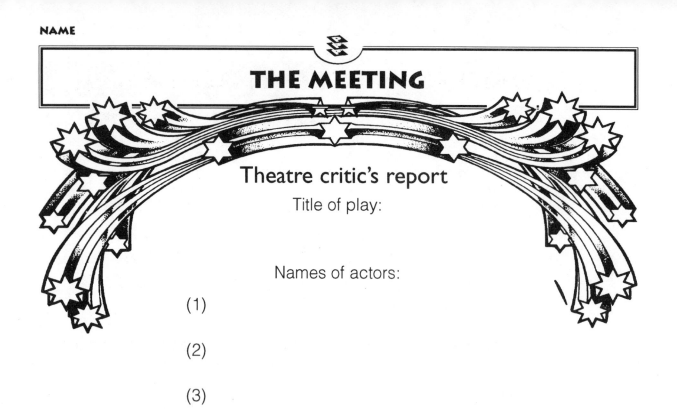

THE MEETING

Theatre critic's report

Title of play:

Names of actors:

(1)

(2)

(3)

The character we found most interesting was...

This character was interesting because...

The best part of the play was when...

We particularly liked this part because...

Suggestions for improving the play:

Out of a total of 5 we give this play _____ marks.

WRITING ABOUT THE MEETING

Dialogue as a play

Mini Monster	Pleased to meet you. I thought I was alone here!
Troll the Terrible	I'm glad you're here. There are others here too. We should have a party. By the way, this is Big Boots.
Mini Monster	I certainly know how you came to have a name like that! Hello.
Big Boots	Isn't this place weird? Full of paper. Never seen so much paper in my life.
Troll the Terrible	To get back to that party...what do you both think?
Mini Monster/ Big Boots (together)	Yes! Great idea. We'll invite all the other monsters lurking around here to come too!

Dialogue as part of a narrative

The monster shuffled across the room and, holding out her hand, roared, 'Pleased to meet you. I thought I was alone here!' Smiling pleasantly, Troll the Terrible replied, 'I'm glad you're here. There are others here too. We should have a party. By the way, this is Big Boots.'

'I certainly know how you came to have a name like that! Hello,' said Mini Monster, gazing in wonder at Big Boots' feet. Big Boots smiled, 'Isn't this place weird? Full of paper. Never seen so much paper in my life.'

'To get back to that party,' interrupted Troll the Terrible, 'what do you both think?'

'Yes! Great idea,' exclaimed Mini Monster and Big Boots in unison, 'We'll invite all the other monsters lurking around here to come too!'

THE STORY OF THE FEAST

Monster parade

This could open with the arrival of the guests.

Where in your school will the feast be held?

How will the guests be announced?

Choose three of the guests to describe in detail?

What decorations can you imagine in place?

What sort of lighting will monsters have for the feast?

What music will be playing?

How will you end this part of the story?

- -

Monster feast

How will you open this part of the story?

In this part you will have to describe the meal.

How do the monsters eat?

Remember to refer to your menu.

Can you think of a joke that the monsters might tell over the meal?

Describe one of the party games played after the meal.

How will this part of the story end?

- -

Monster farewell

The party is nearly over.

Describe the monsters' final dance.

Are they sad to be saying goodbye?

Write two things that they say to show how they feel.

Do they plan ever to return to the school?

Perhaps they will plan to have a reunion somewhere else next year.

How will you end the story?

THE MONSTERS' FEAST – EVALUATION (A)

◆ Please answer the following questions in as mch detail as you can.

There was a mixture of fear and fun in this book.
Which part did you think was most scary? Why?

Which part did you find most fun? Why?

Did the letter at the end of the book sound as if it had been written by the headteacher? Explain your answer.

Where else could the monsters hold their annual celebration?

(1)

(2)

What advice would you offer to the author of this book?

THE MONSTERS' FEAST – EVALUATION (B)

◆ Please answer these questions about the story you have just heard.

	All of it	Most of it	Some of it
Did you enjoy this story?	◯	◯	◯
Was the story well read?	◯	◯	◯
Was the story well illustrated?	◯	◯	◯

Draw or write about the part of the story you enjoyed most.

Did you like the monsters?   YES   NO

Would you like to meet any of them?   YES   NO

Which ones would you like to meet? Why?

_____

_____

Would you like to read or hear another story by this author?   YES   NO

Chapter Seven

PIRATE ADVENTURE

INTRODUCTION

Project description

In this project the children each invent their own pirate character and work in groups of four to write a serial story about what happens when their pirates are shipwrecked. Together the group composes an opening paragraph which sets the scene and then one child is chosen to write the first section of the story. Once this has been written, it is read to the rest of the group, and another child continues and writes what happens next. The final story is published as a group book, written by the four authors, who all play a part in doing the writing, illustrations and putting the publication together.

Why this context?

Most children are familiar with pirate stories and enjoy inventing and describing their own pirate to others in the group. The group responsibility for the book means that all writers are supported by peers who have an equally deep knowledge of the story and a vested interest in helping to ensure high quality work. The serial pattern of individual writing followed by group discussion encourages writers to look for consistency and balance in the characters and the plot as well as to give, and respond to, helpful advice.

This context is good for encouraging children to think beyond stereotypes and create individual characters, with distinct histories, personalities and friendships. Margaret Mahy's *The Man Whose Mother Was a Pirate*, included in this workshop, is a fine example of a story with a very strong pirate central character. Writers are encouraged to think about how to write cliff-hangers and how these contribute to the overall structure of the story. Finally, in considering the ingredients of a good ending and the possible endings for their own story the children consider an aspect of story writing that is not often tackled in individual story-writing contexts.

Project organisation

The children are put into groups of four and everyone is set the task of inventing and making a pirate character. After describing their character to the other group members, the children individually write up a character study, which forms a prologue to the story. The children in each group work individually, and then as a group, to draft the opening sentences of the story, describing the scene of the shipwreck. Then, one individual offers to write what happens, possibly as homework, while other members are finishing their character studies and mounting them on to card. Once finished, this is read to the group, altered in the light of their comments and copied on to A3 paper (with illustration if required) while the next instalment is drafted by someone else. This pattern of individual work presented to the group for comment continues until all the group members have written at least one section. The children work either individually or as a group to craft the most appropriate ending(s).

Publication and presentation

The story is written on to plain A3 paper, which is mounted on to card, leaving a broad border to make a 'big book' format. Each book is read by one of the authors to another group, who must identify areas of particular effectiveness and record these on the evaluation sheet on photocopiable page 84.

Books the children may find useful

Blackbeard the Pirate by Victor Ambrus (Oxford University Press)
Tilly Mint and the Dodo by Berlie Doherty (Collins)
Pirates by Colin Hawkins and Jacqui Hawkins (Armada)
The Great Piratical Rumbustification by Margaret Mahy (Dent)
Horrendous Hullabaloo by Margaret Mahy (Hamish Hamilton)
Pirates by Colin McNaughton (Walker)
Jolly Roger by Colin McNaughton (Walker)
One-eyed Jake by Pat Hutchins (Penguin)
Treasure of Cosy Cove by Tony Ross (Red Fox)
Captain Teachum's Buried Treasure by Peter Carter (Oxford University Press)

PIRATES

Teaching content

Creating characters.

What you need

Collage materials, pieces of paper (12 x 8cm), photocopiable page 80, writing materials.

What to do

Put the children into groups of three or four and ask them each to invent and make a pirate figure on one of the pieces of paper. Explain that the figure should take up the whole area and that it is often easier to stick the collage materials straight on to the paper rather than drawing the figure first.

Tell the children that these pirates live on the same ship and that, as they work, they should think about the following background details for their pirate:

- What is your pirate called?
- How long has he or she been a pirate?
- What did he or she do before becoming a pirate and how did he or she get into piracy?
- What is your pirate's dominant characteristic – is he/she grumpy, cheerful, lazy, happy-go-lucky?
- What does your pirate enjoy or hate about being on a ship for long periods of time?
- What does your pirate enjoy or hate about being on land?
- Does your pirate have any hobbies or interests?
- What was your pirate's greatest triumph or disaster?
- One secret thing that nobody else knows about your pirate.

These questions are listed on photocopiable page 80 with room for the children's notes.

Tell the children to discuss their own pirates and encourage them to help each other with ideas. While the children work, go around the class asking your own questions, such as:

- How did the pirate come by that beautiful earring?
- How did s/he lose his/her leg/hand/eye?
- What jobs or skills does each pirate have?
- What sort of voice does the pirate have?
- How would the pirate explain key events in his/her past? And so on.

Once the pirate collages have been made, ask the children to introduce their character to the rest of their group by sharing key answers to the questions. The children will enjoy divulging their pirate's secret. Then explain that, as with any close-knit group, there are some rivalries and some people are better friends than others. Which pirates in their group get on particularly well, and which are slightly more wary of each other? Why?

2

ALL ABOARD!

Teaching content

- Writing a character study.
- Writing to a time limit.

What you need

Lined paper (A5), plain paper (A3), pirate collages, writing materials, large pieces of card (about 4cm larger all round than A3 paper), questions from previous lesson (if required), glue, scissors.

What to do

Explain that the children will now have a limited amount of time to write a brief character description of their pirate. Explain that this will form the introduction to the book and it is their opportunity to give the reader a good idea of their pirate's character. Encourage them to use questions from the previous activity to structure their writing, adding any further details or incidents from their pirate's past at the end. Let the children write in silence for 15–20 minutes.

When the children have finished their descriptions, give each group a piece of A3 paper and ask the children to arrange their writing and collage pictures on it, sticking the work into place when they are happy with the arrangement.

Finally they should stick the A3 paper on to a large piece of card, leaving a border all round. This can be decorated with a suitable border design at a later stage.

3

DISASTER!

✝ ⏱10

Teaching content
Choosing items for use later in the story.

What you need
Photocopiable page 81, writing materials.

What to do
Give each child a copy of photocopiable page 81. Explain that there has been a dreadful storm. The ship is sinking and each pirate only has time to grab three items to take with them as they escape from the sinking ship. There is no time to consult anyone else in the group.

Ask each child to select and circle the three items they grab as the ship sinks below the waves. Tell them to store this safely somewhere and to tell no one which items they have taken until after the next lesson.

4

WASHED ASHORE

W ✝ ⏱45

Teaching content
• Beginnings.
• Setting the scene.

What you need
Chalkboard, writing materials.

What to do
Explain that the storm has abated and the shipwrecked pirates have been washed ashore on an island. Ask the class to suggest some things they might see as they open their eyes and look around. The children might suggest some of the following: mountains, woods, trees, rocks, sand, sun, sky, inhabitants, clouds, sea, buildings, animals, other pirates from the ship... Try to generate a class list of about 10–15 things and write them on the board for the children to refer to. Ask each child to select two things and to write a descriptive sentence about each of them.

Now ask the children to get back into their groups, to read their sentences to each other and make a group decision about what the island is like.

Explain that this pirate story is going to begin with a description of the island after the storm. What do the pirates see as they open their eyes and look around? Tell the children to work together to compose an opening paragraph that describes the island scene. They could begin by selecting appropriate sentences from those they have written – adding, combining or adapting them if necessary. You may wish to appoint a 'scribe' for each group for this task.

Explain that you don't mind how long the opening paragraph is, but stipulate that it must contain at least one sentence or idea from each person in the group and it must not be inconsistent or contradict itself.

Once the paragraphs have been written, one member of each group should read their paragraph aloud to the class. Ask the other children to comment. Does it set the scene well? Which bits do they think are particularly effective? Why? Allow them to make any final changes if they wish.

5

THE ADVENTURE TAKES OFF

Teaching content
- Developing a story.
- Story and character consistency.
- Ending on cliff-hangers.

What you need
Writing materials, photocopiable pages 82 and 83 (if required), pirate descriptions from activity 1, plain A3 paper, large pieces of card, scissors, glue.

What to do
Explain that this is going to be a serial story, in which various chapters are written by several different people. Each of the contributors takes responsibility for a separate instalment, one after the other.

Tell each group to re-read their opening descriptive paragraph and to choose one person to write the first instalment of the story.

Explain that it is this person's responsibility to decide what happens when the pirates wake up and to draft this first part of the story. The person who is chosen, or who volunteers, may have their own ideas or may choose to discuss ideas with the rest of the group. Explain that everyone will have to write at least one part of the story eventually, but that some brave person has to start.

Once this part of the story has been written in draft form, the writer should read it to the rest of the group and let them comment on it. Photocopiable page 82 provides a useful basis for encouraging children to respond helpfully in this activity.

It is as well to negotiate some basic ground rules for all the writers to follow. You may like the class to consider some or all of the following:
- Each instalment must follow on from the last.
- Each instalment should end on a cliff-hanger (you may have to explain this idea to the children, but they are often familiar with it from watching television serials).
- Writers can only kill off their own character.
- Each writer should try to take account of the pirates' personalities and details as described in activity 1;
- Destructive comments on work are not acceptable – any comments should be as helpful as possible.

Once the group has had a chance to comment, the author should copy the story on to plain A3 paper, placing photocopiable page 83 sideways underneath to use the thick black lines as a guide if required. When they have finished, any unused paper should be trimmed off and the writing mounted on to another large piece of card, leaving a border all round.

6
CONTINUING THE STORY

Teaching content
- Developing a story.
- Story and character consistency.
- Ending on cliff-hangers.

What you need
Pirate stories so far, writing materials, photocopiable pages 82 and 83, plain A3 paper, card, scissors, glue.

What to do
Once the first instalment of the story has been written and agreed by the rest of the group, another person should take on the responsibility of writing the next part of the story. Again, once this has been drafted, the author should read it to the rest of the group and ask for comments, using photocopiable page 82 if necessary. Remind the children that the same ground rules apply for this and for all other instalments of the story. Once this instalment has been agreed, the author should write it neatly on to the A3 paper and mount it on to card as before.

Then a third child from the group should write the next section, and so on, until all the children have written at least one section and there are no more children who want to write.

Occasionally the children get into a rut with their writing and each instalment contains, for example, fight after fight. You can break this pattern by:
- banning fights;
- stepping in and writing a section yourself (this can often 'lift' the story and move it on sufficiently to get the group out of its rut);
- specifying a focus for the next instalment – one of the pirates has a birthday; they find something; someone gets lost; something funny happens and so on.

7
ENDING THE STORY

Teaching content
Writing a satisfying ending.

What you need
Photocopiable anthology page 220 (from *Aspects of the Craft of Writing*), pirate stories so far, writing materials.

What to do
Remind the children of the important ingredients of a satisfying ending:
- It ties up all the loose ends.
- It says what happens to the characters in the future.
- It must be in keeping with what has gone before.

It is sometimes difficult for the children to decide how to end their stories. Give each group a copy of photocopiable anthology page 220 from *Aspects of the Craft of Writing*. This shows several different endings to children's books, and it should give the children an idea of some of the options.

Depending on how the children have worked in their group, you may decide simply to explain that the story now has to end and let the children in each group work together to plan a satisfying ending, choosing one person to write it up. The children usually have a good idea of who has done the most or the least writing towards this story and can use this as an opportunity to make sure that every member of the group does their fair share

Alternatively, if the children find this sort of collaborative work difficult, ask all the children to read the story so far and each to draft their own ending. These can then be:
• shared among the group who should, together, choose the best to be copied out for the story, justifying their choice;
• all included at the end of the book as alternative endings.

DECIDING A TITLE, FINISHING THE WORK

Teaching content

Presentation.

What you need

Pirate stories, collage materials, card for front cover, writing and art materials.

What to do

Once the stories have been finished, the groups should decide on a title, either by common consent or by each writing a title, sharing their ideas and selecting the best. They should also decide on the following, making sure that the work is evenly divided:
• one or two people to make the front cover listing important details such as the title, authors and publisher;
• one or two people to organise and collate a dedication page in which each author dedicates the work to someone who is important to them;
• one or two people to decorate the borders;
• one person to write blurb and author details for the back cover.

It is a good idea to ask the children to decide who will do each job and to record this on a sheet of paper, which they hand to the teacher or keep in a safe place, so that everyone has

something to remind them about what has been agreed in terms of work. The activities in the presentation chapter can be used to support aspects of this work as required.

CELEBRATION AND REVIEW

Teaching content

• Consideration of another group's story.
• Presentation.

What you need

Pirate books, photocopiable page 84, writing materials, photocopiable page 172 (optional).

What to do

When all the groups have finished their pirate books, each group should appoint a reader to present and read the book to another group. Let the readers practise reading aloud to a partner if they wish, possibly using the evaluation sheet from the presentation chapter (photocopiable page 172). Other readers may prefer to practise reading the story on their own or to a friend or parent at home.

When the time comes for the readings to take place, sit each group in a different area of the classroom. Each group's reader should move with the book to another group, leaving the remaining group members as the listeners for a new story. When the readers have finished reading the story, they may return to their own groups, leaving the book behind for discussion.

Give each group a copy of photocopiable page 84 and tell them to discuss the book thoroughly. They should appoint:
• a chairperson to ensure that everyone contributes and that all comments are kind and respect the effort that has been put into the publication;
• a scribe to record the comments on the photocopiable sheet;
• a reporter who will return the book and report the group's comments to the writing group.

Remind them that your focus is on the insight they show as readers – you are looking for helpful and encouraging comments that recognise the strengths of the publication under discussion.

PIRATES

• Answer the following questions about the pirate you have created.

1. What is your pirate called?

2. How long has he or she been a pirate?

3. What did he or she do before becoming a pirate and how did he or she get into piracy?

4. What is your pirate's dominant characteristic
    – is he/she grumpy, cheerful, lazy, happy-go-lucky...?

5. What does your pirate enjoy or hate about being on a ship for long periods of time?

6. What does your pirate enjoy or hate about being on land?

7. Does your pirate have any hobbies or interests?

8. What was your pirate's greatest triumph or disaster?

9. One secret thing that nobody else knows about your pirate.

DISASTER!

◆ You only have time to grab three of these items before your ship sinks. Which will you take with you?

television
comics
money
rope
spade
tent
toothpaste and toothbrush
passport
watch
clean clothes
binoculars
compass
knife
blankets
torch
matches
food and provisions
gift for friendly inhabitants
map

◆ Do not tell anyone which items you have chosen.

THE ADVENTURE TAKES OFF

Group names: **Date:**

Author's name:

Group response

Does the passage make sense, considering what has happened earlier?

Are the events described clearly?

Are the characters consistent?

Does the story end on a cliff-hanger?

The best thing about this story is:

One thing the author may like to reconsider is:

- -

Author's response

I found these comments:

helpful	☐☐☐☐☐☐☐☐☐	unhelpful
supportive	☐☐☐☐☐☐☐☐☐	destructive
clear	☐☐☐☐☐☐☐☐☐	unclear

THE ADVENTURE TAKES OFF: GUIDE LINES

◆ Place this page under your writing paper so that you can write along the lines. The box at the beginning allows you to draw an illuminated initial letter if you wish.

CELEBRATION AND REVIEW

Book title:

Authors:

First thoughts on looking at the front cover of the book are that:

What we particularly like about the pirate characters is that:

Our comments on the story are:

Our comments on the ending are:

What we liked about the presentation was:

One thing about this book that we wish we had done in ours was:

Reviewers' signatures:

Scholastic
WRITING
Workshop

Chapter Eight

CASTLES
IN THE AIR

INTRODUCTION

Project description

In this project children write a fairy story for younger children in the school. The story is set in a castle. Each child makes a castle and then decides what sort of castle it will be. The children make, and thereby invent, the main character who inhabits the castle and then, something happens...

Through the early activities in this project, the children clarify the important aspects of audience, character, place and problem and are in an excellent position to write a first draft of the story. Later, individual teacher–child conferences help them to re-draft and edit their work before publishing it in the form of 'castle' books, complete with lift-the-flap illustrations, illuminated letters and borders.

The authors read their stories to younger children in the school who then complete an evaluation form to provide a permanent memory and celebration of the event.

Why this context?

All children are familiar with fairy stories and are able to discuss the sort of characters and events that drive them. The project encourages children to think about the needs of a very different audience, but one with whom they are all familiar.

The project offers strong support in creating characters, reading stories aloud with expression and in celebrating writing. Children are asked to consider typical fairy-story opening sentences and to write a magical beginning for their own story. It provides an opportunity for the teacher to act as a writing partner and both to model and to teach through the conferencing process.

Project organisation

The initial work consists of whole-class lessons in which children work as individuals or with writing partners to make the castle books, create characters and plan the story events. Once the basic planning decisions have been made, the children can begin writing their first drafts of their stories. As these are finished children move at their own rate to tackle a variety of presentation tasks, while the teacher holds writing conferences with individuals. Finally, the children work with writing partners to practise reading aloud and eventually present their stories to younger children in the school.

Publication and presentation format

The story is published in the form of a 'castle' book which opens out to form a three-dimensional model of a castle. The book is read by the author to one or two children from an infant class, who are asked to complete a specially-designed reader response form.

Books the children may find useful

Geoffrey Strangeways by Jill Murphy (Walker Books)
Sir Gawain and the Loathly Lady edited by Selina Hastings (Walker Books)
King of the Castle by Mary Hoffman (Hamish Hamilton)
Visit to Folly Castle by Nina Beachcroft (Mammoth)

1

INFANT STORIES

Teaching content

• Awareness of audience.
• The needs of a particular audience (younger readers).

What you need

Writing materials, chalkboard.

What to do

A sense of audience is crucial for good writing and children need to be clear about who will read their stories and what implications this may have for their writing. This activity provides a focus for thinking about the qualities six- and seven-year-old children look for and enjoy, and the children should remember them when they plan and write their stories. It also encourages children to use their own experience as readers to improve their writing.

Begin by explaining that one of the infant teachers has told you how much her class loves stories. Now tell your class that they are going to write stories for the younger children in the school which, once finished, will be read aloud to children in an infant class. Before beginning to write, however, it is important to think carefully about the sorts of books and stories young children enjoy.

Ask the children to write down the name of a story they remember liking when they were six or seven years old. If they cannot remember one let them go to the library for inspiration. They should pick out a book they think would be suitable for that age group - this may be anything from a fairy tale to something they have seen on television. Then, ask them to write down one particular thing they liked about that story. It may have been:

• a character;
• an exciting event;
• the way the story ended;
• because the story was funny/sad/frightening;
• because the story was set in a beautiful/mysterious place;
• because they liked the magic or the adventure.

Ask the children to share their responses with the class and record on the board why they found the stories memorable. Explain that when the children write their stories, they should try to include those qualities that made stories enjoyable for them.

Now tell the class that, over the next few weeks, they will each be writing a story for the infants. The stories will be set in, or around, a castle. When writing and publishing their books, the children must remember all the points that have been discussed.

2

THE CASTLE

✝→ⓦ→✝✝ ㊵

Teaching content

• Brainstorming possibilities.
• Writers make choices.

What you need

One sample castle, photocopiable page 95, A2-sized sheets of paper, chalkboard, writing materials.

What to do

Use the instructions on photocopiable page 95 to make a sample castle before the lesson. Show this to the class, explaining how the pages work and demonstrating how it opens out to form a castle. Then, give out the paper and photocopiable page 95 and help the children each to make a castle.

With the whole class, brainstorm what sort of castle this could be. Record all suggestions on the board and encourage as wide a range of ideas as possible. This session sets the tone for the rest of the project. Don't be disheartened if early suggestions lack imagination; one class, who produced delightful books, offered initial brainstorm suggestions such as 'brick', 'stone' and 'brown'. It is very important that *all* contributions are accepted and that *every* idea, no matter how pedestrian, is recorded on the board. Try to make a positive comment about each one. Remember that for each child who volunteers an idea there will be three or four who have ideas which they *may* contribute depending on how you respond. When there is a good flow of ideas you can occasionally add your own suggestions, writing these on the board along with those from the children. Finally, ask the children each to select one type of castle on which to base their story.

Arrange the class in writing pairs. Give each pair a large sheet of paper and ask them to brainstorm words associated with each type of castle they have chosen. Make a temporary 'work in progress' display of these, ensuring that they are placed at a level at which the children can read them. Tell the writing pairs that they should add words to their sheet as and when they think of them.

MAKING THE CHARACTERS

Teaching content
Developing characterisation.

What you need
Paper squares (10x10 cm), glue, exciting collage materials: sequins, feathers, foil and so on.

What to do
Give each child a square of paper. Tell the children that they are to use the collage materials to make the character who lives in their castle. This character, when finished, will be stuck behind the first page of the castle book, to be revealed when the door on page 1 is opened.

Explain that the character might be human, but it could be a creature or a magical being. The most important thing is that it should appeal to the young children who will eventually be reading the book and that it should fit with the sort of castle the children have chosen to write about.

Emphasise that the children *must* make the character the size of the piece of paper, no bigger or smaller. Advise the children to work directly from the collage materials, rather than drawing the character first.

While the children are making their characters, ask them to think about the following aspects, which should be written up on the board. (This thinking time is extremely valuable when children come to write about their characters in the next session.)
- The character's name
- The character's age
- One thing the character likes or dislikes
- One favourite pastime
- One weakness or strength
- One thing that has happened to the character in the past
- One secret thing about the character that nobody knows
- How the character behaves when angry, frightened, pleased...

Once the characters have been made, explain that each child will have two minutes to tell their writing partner about the character they have created. Remind the class after one minute, and after two minutes use a prearranged sign to get them to stop. Before swapping over, give the listening partners an opportunity to ask questions, if they haven't already, in order to help both children clarify and build up a complete and detailed picture of the character.

End by telling the children to continue thinking about their castles and their characters: how the characters came to live in the castle, what they do all day and what they like and dislike about living there.

DOORWAYS

Teaching content
Firming up the castle description.

What you need
Photocopiable page 96, collage and colouring materials, scissors, adhesive.

What to do
Show the class the 'castle exemplar' you made and explain that on page 1 of the story there will be a door that can open to reveal the main character. The door can be any sort of opening at all, depending on the type of castle or their character. It may be the main castle door, a dungeon door or a trap door. Show the children

While the children work, take the opportunity to help individual children to visualise and describe their castle by asking questions:
• What sort of door are they making and why?
• What does the castle look like from the outside?
• What does the castle look like from the inside?
• What are the wider surroundings like?
• Who lives in the castle?
• Who visits it regularly/occasionally, and why?

5

WHAT HAPPENS?

ṫ-ṫṫ ⏱⃝20

Teaching content
Planning a storyline.

What you need
Photocopiable page 97, writing materials.

What to do
Each child now has a very clear picture of the main character and the type of castle that will dominate her story. The next step is to help the children plan something dramatic that happens at the castle. What is it? It could be a strange visitor, a sound during the night or something magical. Whatever happens will mark the starting point for the story.

Ask the children to consider the questions on photocopiable page 97. Explain that only some of them will apply to individual castles or characters and ask the children to tick those that are applicable to their own, jotting brief notes (maybe just one or two words) about their ideas beside the questions. Then ask the children to explain their sheet briefly to their writing partners, who should help them to elaborate on ideas or contribute new ones.

End by explaining that the children now have lots of possible ideas for their stories, but it is their important decision to choose one that will form the basis of their story. Remind them that the story is for infants and that this should be one of the considerations they bear in mind when deciding which idea to follow up. Tomorrow, they must come with a firm idea for their story which they will record on the bottom section of the photocopiable sheet.

the pictures of doors on photocopiable page 96 and discuss them with the class. List the possible types of door furniture: hinges, handles, bell push/pulls, spy holes, nameplates and so on. Each child must think about his own castle and character and design and make an appropriate door and door furniture.

The children must choose where their door will be situated on the first page. They should draw around their character figures to be sure that the character will fit behind the door. The door should be drawn very exactly using a special pen line to indicate which sides are to open and which therefore will be cut. Ask writing partners to ensure that only the top sheet of paper is cut, leaving the bottom sheet untouched so that children do not accidentally cut around the whole door shape, making the doors fall out rather than fold open. The door can be decorated using collage and colouring materials and characters carefully stuck behind so that they are revealed when the doors are opened.

OPENINGS

W ✝ 25

Teaching content
Descriptive writing.

What you need
Photocopiable anthology page 219 (from *Aspects of the Craft of Writing*), chalkboard, writing materials.

What to do
By now the children should have a clear idea about what their castle is like and they will have thought about (and briefly recorded on photocopiable page 97 in the previous activity) what will happen in their story. This activity helps them to find a way of starting their story and gives them another period of time spent thinking about what happens.

Begin by asking the class to consider the opening sentences on the photocopiable anthology page. Which ones could be the opening sentences to some of the favourite stories mentioned in activity 1? Can they remember the opening sentence of their own favourite story? Elicit as many suggestions for opening sentences as possible and write them on the board for the whole class to see.

Ask the children to think about their own castle, character and story while reading all the beginnings carefully (both from the photocopiable sheet and the list generated by the class). Then, ask them to write a suitable beginning and first paragraph for their own story. Explain that they may begin their paragraph by copying one of the opening sentences verbatim, combining parts from several sentences, adding their own ideas to an opening sentence or by writing their own completely new sentence.

End the lesson by explaining that tomorrow the children will start the rest of their story. Between now and tomorrow, the children should think about what happens and how they are going to relate this to the young children who will read their books.

DRAFTING THE STORY

✝ 60

Teaching content
Drafting the story.

What you need
Writing materials.

What to do
The children have now been thoroughly prepared for writing their stories. Explain that this is a first draft and you want the children to use the next hour to tell the story in the most exciting way possible. It is helpful to remind children of the re-drafting and editing advice given in the Introduction to this volume and of what to do if they don't know how to spell a word. Discuss how long their stories might be by getting them to look at the number of pages and the amount of writing space on the castle books. Remind them that the front and back pages will not be used for the story and that

illustrations will also take up space. Explain that additional pages can be added if absolutely necessary, so it doesn't matter if the story is long. Remind them also that length does not always indicate quality and not to worry if their story is shorter or longer than somebody else's.

Tell the children that, for this story, you will be the initial writing partner for everyone. This first writing session will be conducted in silence to ensure that everyone gets uninterrupted time for writing. Later you will arrange to read and discuss their stories with them and will help in the revision process.

Allow this session and any other time required for actually writing the story. Put a special tray or box in the classroom to contain the children's self-corrected work.

8

THE WRITING CONFERENCE

Teaching content
- Audience.
- Individual tuition on writing strategies and techniques.
- How to be a writing partner.

What you need
Child's story, photocopiable page 98, drawing and collage materials, adhesive, scissors, photocopiable pages 166–168..

What to do
Discussing writing with individual children is crucial, but takes a long time. The section on conferencing in the Introduction to this volume gives advice on how to conduct a writing conference. To make time for individual conferences with the teacher, the children should start the activities listed below as soon as their first draft is complete and placed in the special tray or box provided:
- borders
- illuminated letters
- posters
- illustrations for the inside walls of the castle
The presentation chapter contains useful activities to help children produce borders, illuminated letters and advertising posters for their books. To design the inside of the castle walls, show the children how to build up the

picture by drawing first the main features and details that are appropriate for the type of castle. For example, a traditional castle might have pictures, tapestries, cobwebs, pans hanging round the fire, and so on. Finally show how the spaces may be filled with stonework or wall coverings. To ensure that the walls will be drawn the right way up, tell the children to draw lightly small arrows pointing upwards on all four walls before they open out their castle books to start.

Make a list showing the order in which you will see the children for writing conferences. A knowledge of the children, or a quick glance through the first drafts, will give you an idea of how much help different children will require. Arrange to see a variety of children during each session – some who require more and some who require less time. A list showing the order in which you will see children will help to ensure that you see the whole class. Photocopiable page 98 may help you and the child to keep useful records of these consultations.

WRITING OUT THE STORY

† ○

Teaching content

- Presentation.
- Handwriting.

What you need

Castle books, writing and illustration/collage materials, plain paper cut to suitable shapes for illustrations, lined paper cut to castle-book size for writing out the story.

What to do

When the children are ready to begin copying stories into books they must plan which sections will be illustrated. Some children are helped if the teacher specifies an ideal number of pictures (for example, 4–6). The children should go through the stories and put lines, or stars, at the points where illustrations will be useful. They can discuss this with writing partners, if necessary. Ask the children to look at their castle books and work out:

- how many pages they will have for writing;
- which illustrations are required and where they should go;
- how much writing should go on each page.

This is an important planning stage for any publication. The children are being taught a process that they will be able to use when publishing in the future. It is important to have an initial skeletal plan, although plans made now will, of course, be changed as they are implemented, just as writers change ideas as they progress.

Point out the various sizes and shapes of paper for illustrations. Stress that the pictures need not go at the top or bottom of pages and that sometimes writing can be done around the illustrations. Suggest that the children select the paper for all the illustrations at the start. Explain that, having chosen the size and shape of the illustrations they may decide for themselves when to copy out the story and when to illustrate. If their copying out is ahead of their illustrating they will know how much space to leave; they will also be free to illustrate a section they have not yet copied out, gluing their picture into place when they have copied out that part of the story.

FINISHING OFF

†·†† ⑨⓪

Teaching content

- Deciding on a title.
- Putting the finishing touches to a project.

What you need

Castle books, writing and illustration/collage materials.

What to do

When most of the children have finished the writing and the first child has finished all the other work to be done, tell the children they now have to decide on a good title for their story and create a cover for their book. Remind them that a good title indicates something about the content and type of story, but most importantly, it engages the reader's interest and imagination. The title works together with other items on the cover of a book to encourage the prospective reader to pick it up. The activities in the presentation chapter on features of book covers may provide useful guidance for the children.

The children should also write an author biography and a blurb for the back cover of their books. These items are also covered in the presentation chapter. You may want to ensure that writers are reading and learning from the work of their peers. One simple way to encourage this without labouring the point, is to ask each author to write the blurb for someone else's book.

CELEBRATION AND REVIEW

Teaching content
- Reading aloud.
- Audience.
- Self esteem.

What you need
Y2/3 children, castle books, photocopiable pages 99 and 100.

What to do
At the start of the project you will have arranged for the children to read their finished story to one or two children from an infant class. At this point, each author should be given the names of the children to whom they will be reading. The date for the readings should be set about one week hence.

Explain that the children will need to write formal invitations to the younger children for whom the books have been written. Use the activity in the presentation chapter to help them to do this.

The children must appreciate that they will have to read their stories well if young children are going to listen to them. If the listeners cannot hear or understand they will switch off. Explain that they will need to practise reading aloud and can help each other in this respect. The presentation chapter contains an activity and evaluation sheet to help with this.

Immediately before the reading session, spend some time explaining carefully the importance of approaching young children with respect and kindness. The older children must introduce themselves to the younger children and thank them for coming to listen to the story. Suggest that the authors begin by showing the book, pointing out the illustrations and demonstrating how the book stands up. They will need to explain about the main character and what sort of castle this is. Warn them that they must be prepared to let the younger children touch the books, turning pages, opening doors and exploring the inside.

Photocopiable pages 99 and 100 can be used for the listeners to record their responses to the stories. It would be helpful if infant teachers spoke to the children about the advantages of positive reviews – it is very easy to upset a tender, young author.

THE CASTLE

How to make the castle book

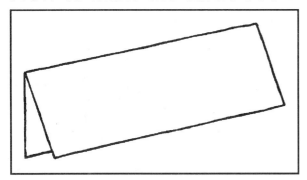

1. Fold the paper in half lengthways.

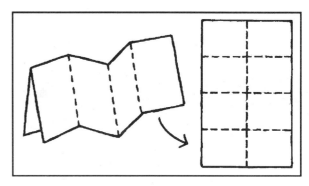

2. Fold the paper twice more, so that if you opened it out there would be eight sections.

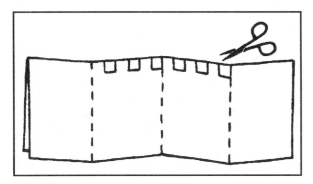

3. First draw, then cut out, the crenellations of the castle in the middle two sections.

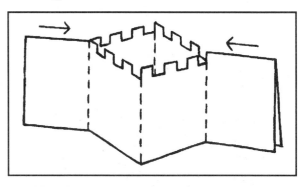

4. Hold the paper lengthways. Push the left and right ends towards the middle. The castle should open out.

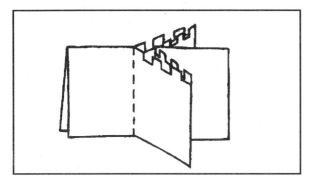

5. Continue pushing the ends together until the castle space in the middle closes up. Close the end sections around to form a book.

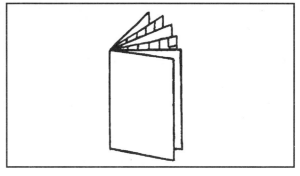

6. Add additional pages by taping another piece of paper folded as in the diagram. Cut off any sections not required.

NB: The idea and details of how to make this origami book come from *A Book of One's Own*, by Paul Johnson, Hodder & Stoughton, 1990.

DOORWAYS

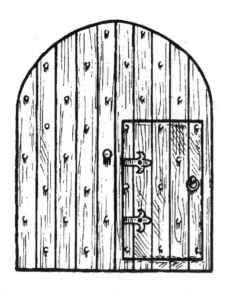

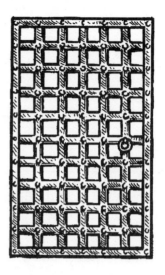

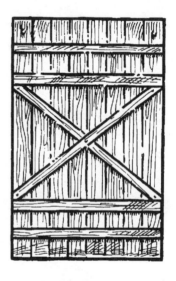

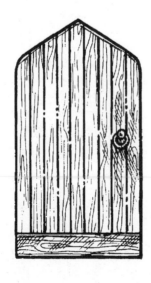

Scholastic
IMAGINATIVE WRITING
Workshop

WHAT HAPPENS?

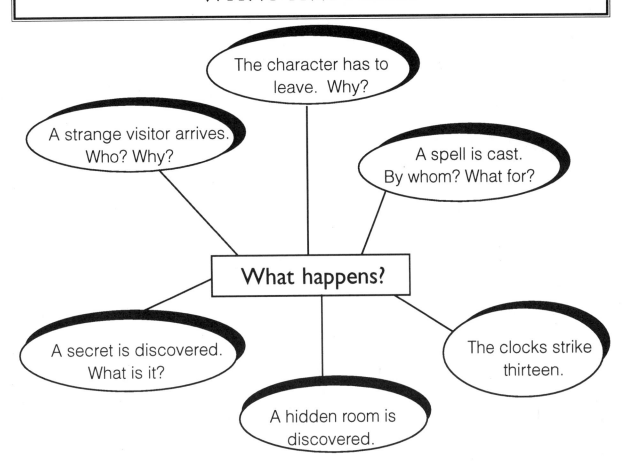

The character has to leave. Why?

A strange visitor arrives. Who? Why?

A spell is cast. By whom? What for?

What happens?

A secret is discovered. What is it?

The clocks strike thirteen.

A hidden room is discovered.

What happens is...

THE WRITING CONFERENCE

In the conference we discussed:

The author is going to think about:

Author's name: _____

Date: _____

In the conference we discussed:

The author is going to think about:

Author's name: _____

Date: _____

Scholastic
IMAGINATIVE WRITING
Workshop

CELEBRATION AND REVIEW

Title of book: _____

Author: _____

Listener/reader: _____

Colour the face.

	a lot	a little	not much
Did you like this story?	☺	😐	☹
Did you like the way it was read?	☺	😐	☹
Did you like the cover?	☺	😐	☹
Did you like the pictures?	☺	😐	☹
Would you like to hear another story?	☺	😐	☹

Which part of the story did you like best?

Draw a picture of the best part.

Write about the best part.

_____

_____

_____

_____

_____

CELEBRATION AND REVIEW

◆ Draw a picture of the best character in the story.

◆ This character is having a birthday. Draw a picture of the gift you would like to give this character.

Scholastic
WRITING
Workshop

Chapter Nine

STAR MYTH

INTRODUCTION

Project description

In this project, the children are asked to write myths about imaginary star constellations and to make a 'talking book' story tape to accompany a written version of the story.

The project begins by explaining what makes a myth different from other types of story and gives the children two examples of myths that 'explain' real star constellations. The children are shown how many story-tellers and writers plan by using a series of pictures to capture the main events in sequence, along with some key vocabulary or phrases. One of the star constellation myths is used to provide a worked example of this. The other myth can be used for children to extract their own main events and invent some key vocabulary and phrases to use in telling the story orally to their partner.

The children are then given an imaginary constellation of a horse and are asked to work in groups of three to invent a myth explaining the constellation, draw the key events in their story along with the words and phrases that will help them to tell it effectively. This is used as the basis for an oral story-telling session.

Finally, the children work individually to invent a myth for an imaginary star constellation, either choosing one from the selection on photocopiable page 110 or inventing their own. They map the story and think about how to tell it before writing it down. The final version of the story is read or told to the rest of the class in a candlelit story-telling session.

Why this context?

Through this context, children are introduced to the origins and structures of a myth. They learn that myths explain social or physical phenomena and must begin with the question 'why?' In keeping with the oral tradition from which myths spring, the children are encouraged to tell the story orally before writing it down, and are given opportunities to practise story-telling both individually and in groups.

The process of mapping the main events of a story and recording key vocabulary and phrases offers children a new approach to planning. They come to see the written story as merely one way of jogging the story-teller's memory. The emphasis on oral story-telling also encourages children to think about how to present stories effectively, and the evaluation sheet helps them to focus on how to do this.

The presentation of the stories in different ways, as Big Books, as tapes or 'talking books' and as oral stories to be told to a live audience, encourages children to think about the skills and processes involved in each different aspect of presentation. Children often surprise themselves about the advantages of different forms of delivery, which form they find most enjoyable and which aspects of each are particularly challenging and why. It is also true that talking books are becoming increasingly popular and can provide a powerful motivating force for some children.

Myths as a special type of story often fascinate children and this project can be extended into writing all sorts of myths simply by asking the children to write lists of questions about natural phenomena and social customs. They may, for example, ask 'Why do people have different colours of skin, hair, eyes?', 'Why does the moon only shine at night?', 'Where does the sun go when it goes down?', 'Why is the grass green?' Each question can generate a story that can be invented, mapped, told and recorded as described in this project and published either in a Big Book of myths or in individual books.

Project organisation

The children begin working in pairs to read two myths and plan out the main events and identify key story-telling vocabulary and phrases for one of them. They then work in different groups of three to invent, plan a story sequence and practise telling a myth about a new imaginary star constellation in the shape of a horse. The project ends with individual story-telling and writing of myths based on imaginary star constellations either chosen from a photocopiable sheet or invented by the child.

Publication and presentation

These stories are published in the form of story tapes, along with a class 'Big Book' collection of stories. Wallpaper sample books are very useful for this. Illustrations and stories may be stuck on to sample pages, which provide ready-made borders for the work. New covers can be stuck on to the front and title details may be added to the spine. The books can be kept in the school library or a central display area for other children and visitors to read.

It is useful to have a supply of short, blank cassettes on to which the children can record their talking books. The tapes accompanying the Big Class Book should have beautiful inlay cards to fit inside each plastic cassette box.

Finally, the teacher needs to arrange for a series of candlelit story-sessions in which these stories can be told to the rest of the class.

Books the children may find useful

How the Birds Changed Their Feathers by Joanna Troughton (Penguin)
How the Rabbit Stole the Fire by Joanna Troughton (Penguin)
Folk Tales of the World series (Penguin)

1

READING THE STARS
†·†† ⑤⓪

Teaching content

- What is a myth.
- Mapping a story.

What you need

Photocopiable pages 106 and 107, drawing materials.

What to do

Explain that in the days when there were no books, radio or television, people provided their own entertainment by inventing and telling stories. Before they were written down, stories were kept alive by being told and re-told regularly. It is from this oral tradition that myths spring. Myths were the stories told by people long ago to explain natural phenomena or the development of social customs. Myths were told to explain all sorts of things but one of the most popular subjects was star constellations. The Greeks saw pictures in the star clusters in the sky and interpreted these as being heroes or favoured animals who had been placed forever in the sky by the gods for different reasons.

Give each child a copy of photocopiable pages 106 and 107 and ask them to read the short story explanations that go with the two star constellations on photocopiable page 106. Explain that many reference books about astronomy relate the myths about each constellation, as well as the scientific information.

Tell the children that story-tellers often map their stories in picture form. This helps to clarify the main points and order the ideas. Sometimes they will add words and phrases that are essential to the storyline. The story-teller can use this plan as a memory jogger during the story-telling session.

Ask the children to look at the top half of photocopiable page 107 which shows a map for the first star story on photocopiable page 106. Draw attention to how it has been organised. Ask the children to choose the main points from the second star story and to draw a similar story map for that at the bottom of photocopiable page 107. Then arrange the children in pairs and ask them to use the maps in order to tell the second story to each other.

2

THE HORSE CONSTELLATION
††† ⑥⓪

Teaching content

- Creating a myth.
- Mapping the main events of a story.

What you need

Photocopiable page 108, drawing materials, scissors.

What to do

Organise the class into groups of three and give each group a copy of photocopiable page 108, showing the Horse Constellation. Tell the children that their group is going to create a myth to explain how the Horse Constellation came to be in the sky. Suggest several possibilities, for example, the horse may have done some heroic deed, or perhaps it is running away for some reason, or perhaps it has a particular talent and the gods have chosen to stable it forever in the sky or perhaps it has been banished to the sky as a punishment...

Each group must decide what the character of the horse is like, what the horse has done and how it came to be in the sky.

Explain that each group is going to tell its story to the class and so they must map the main events and add any important words and phrases they may wish to use. These will provide memory joggers for telling the story.

When this task is completed, the map should be cut into three equal parts and distributed among the group members. (If you do not wish to cut up the photocopiable page, photocopy the finished sheet twice and give a copy to each group member.) Each child will tell one part of the story.

The next activity will prepare the children for the story-telling session.

3
RULES FOR GOOD STORY-TELLERS

Teaching content
- Developing good story-telling techniques.
- Devising rules for story-telling.

What you need
Writing materials, large sheets of paper, marker pens.

What to do
Put two groups of three together to form groups of six. Ask the children to think of good story-tellers they know, perhaps a teacher, a parent, a childminder or another child. Tell them to consider the style of this person's delivery and to each jot down two main points about this person's skill as a story-teller. They may refer to the use of voice, ways in which they include specific members of their audience, or their facial expressions, body language or eye-contact.

Tell each group of six to discuss what they have each written and then to write a list of pointers or rules for good story-telling on their large sheet of paper, putting the most important ones at the top.

4
PRACTISING STORY-TELLING

Teaching content
Practising story-telling skills.

What you need
Story maps from activity 2, rules for story-telling from activity 3, a cassette player, a blank cassette, photocopiable page 109.

What to do
Allow the children to practise telling their horse myths, using the rules for story-telling that they devised in the previous activity. Each child in turn should tell his or her own part of the story to the other two. You may like to suggest that they practise this at home first, either in front of a mirror or to a family member. If they wish they could record their story on to a cassette, play it back and evaluate their own story-telling. The presentation chapter contains a useful activity on practising effective story-telling.

They should then 'perform' their story to the other group of three with whom they worked in activity 3 – and vice versa. Use photocopiable page 109 as a useful focus for both self-evaluation and evaluation by others.

TALKING BOOKS

Teaching content

- Writing and illustrating a myth.
- Reading a story.

What you need

Examples of book and tape packages (optional), writing and drawing materials, photocopiable page 110 (for support), gold or silver stars, gold or silver pens, black paper, a cassette recorder, a blank cassette, photocopiable page 109.

What to do

Most children will be familiar with talking books from home, school and libraries. If possible, show them an example of a book and tape packaged together. Explain that the class is going to make a 'Star-Gazer's Talking Book' which will be a compilation of individually written stories and a cassette of these, recorded by individual story-writers/tellers.

Tell the children that they are going to invent a new star pattern in the sky and then create an interesting myth to explain the presence of this constellation in the sky. Children who find it difficult to create their own design may like to choose one from photocopiable page 110.

The children are now familiar with the formula for creating star myths and should be able to draw their constellations and map the main points of their myths. With writing partners, children should exchange their stories, helping each other by questioning inconsistencies or suggesting additions and alterations.

Children now have a map which can be used as a plan for writing the myth. Illustrate the stories with the constellation made from shiny stars or gold or silver pens on black paper. When complete, the myths should be collated in a Big Book and a cover made.

Each child should then practise reading their story aloud before recording it on to the cassette. The cassette box should then be decorated and given a title.

Finally, in the classroom, a traditional story-telling ambience should be created at the end of the day for fifteen minutes and all children given the opportunity to tell their stories over the course of a week. Children could be gathered in a comfortable circle on the carpet in the library, with the story-teller in an armchair. In the gloaming of a winter's day, candles can add the finishing touches, creating the atmosphere of story-telling in the oral tradition. When the story-teller has finished the audience should be given copies of photocopiable page 109 to evaluate the presentation.

READING THE STARS

Star story 1: Corus, the raven

The raven was originally a white bird and was a spy for Apollo. The god would send the raven out to spy on his friends to make sure they were being loyal to him.

On one occasion, the raven brought back to Apollo bad news about his friends. Apollo flew into a rage and cursed the bird, changing it from white to be forever black. He then cast it into the sky to sit on the back of Hydra, a many-headed monster.

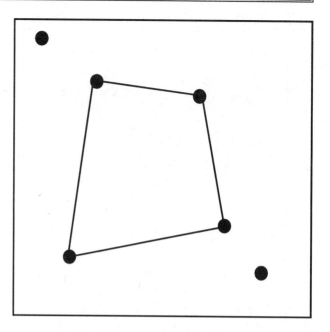

Star story 2: Cygnus, the swan

Cygnus was the best friend of Phaeton, the son of the god Helius, who drove the chariot of the sun around the sky every day.

One day Phaeton begged his father to allow him to drive the chariot across the sky just once and Helius reluctantly agreed to this.

When he set off, all went well until the horses recognised that the hands guiding them were inexperienced. The highly-strung horses became wildly out of control. The chariot drove too close to the Earth and set forests on fire, causing great deserts to be formed. The Earth was threatened with destruction and so Jupiter launched a thunderbolt, throwing Phaeton from his chariot into a deep river. Worried about his friend, Cygnus searched for him in the water, swimming up and down and dipping his head into the river, desperately peering at the river bed. The gods admired his loyalty and turned him into a swan. In this form, Cygnus was transported to heaven. Swans to this day dip their heads in the water, searching the river bed.

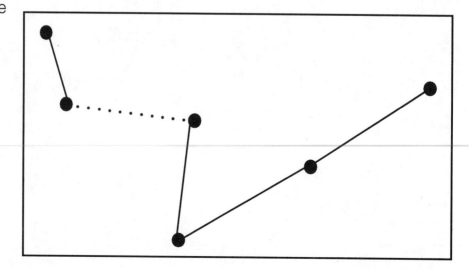

Scholastic
IMAGINATIVE WRITING
Workshop

READING THE STARS

This is a picture map for the story of Corus, the raven.

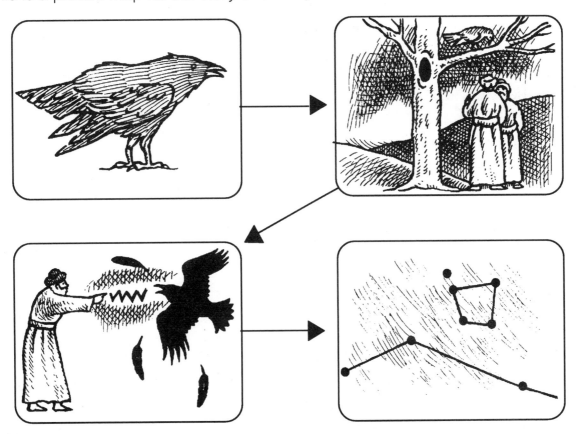

• Now draw your own picture map for the story of Cygnus, the swan.

THE HORSE CONSTELLATION

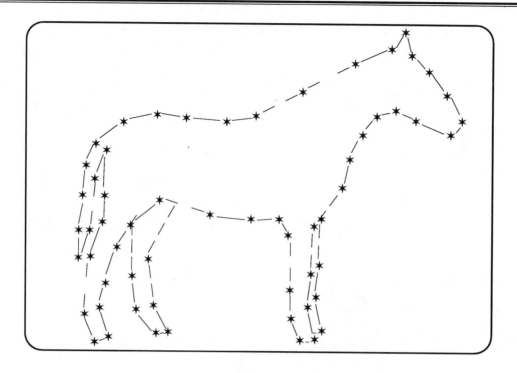

◆ Answer the following questions about the horse above.

1. What is the horse like (character: brave, impetuous, angry...)?

2. What has the horse done?

3. How did the horse come to be in the sky?

◆ Now map your story here.

EVALUATING THE STORY-TELLER.

◆ After listening to the story of the constellation, answer the following questions.

1.   Did the story-teller find a quiet place?

2.   Did the story-teller draw listeners in close?

3.   Did the story-teller find an interesting beginning?

4.   Did the story-teller maintain eye-contact?

5.   Was the story well paced?

6.   Were the volume and tone of voice altered to create interest?

7.   Was the story-teller's voice clear and easy to hear?

One excellent aspect of the story-teller's work...

One piece of advice to improve the story-teller's skill...

TALKING BOOKS

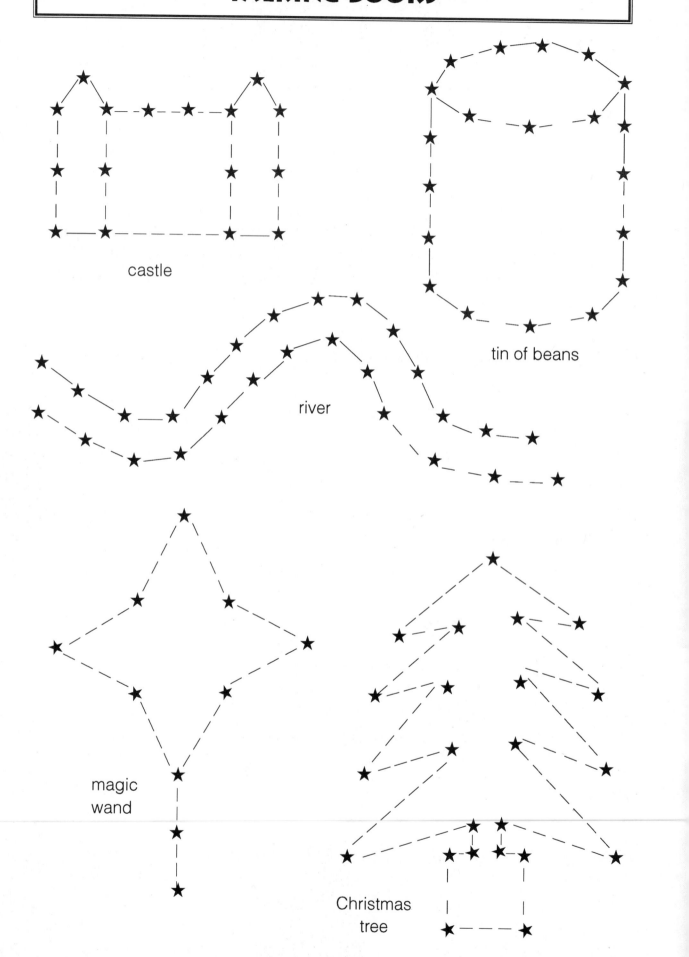

castle

tin of beans

river

magic wand

Christmas tree

Scholastic
IMAGINATIVE WRITING
Workshop

Scholastic WRITING Workshop

Chapter Ten

TRUE STORIES

INTRODUCTION

Project description

In this project the children write a story based on an incident that actually happened to them. They begin by recording on a photocopiable sheet interesting incidents or experiences they have had, either recently or in the distant past. If they so choose, the children may take these sheets home for further discussion with parents or other members of the family, before working in pairs in class to help each other to choose one incident that would make a good story. Each child then has to write a character study of him or herself as seen by others. This is used as the prologue to the story and exemplar material of other writers' work helps children to lead from this into their story, which is planned and written in three parts. The stories are published on card with, if possible, a photograph of the author at the appropriate age. The story is read to and commented on by an adult who knows the child and may well be familiar with the incident on which the story is based.

Why this context?

Many writers draw upon personal experience in their work, either by incorporating events and characters from their own lives into the stories they are writing or by basing whole stories on events they have experienced. This project introduces children to the idea of drawing on real characters and their own life experiences for story-writing. It encourages children to step back from the experience and cast themselves, their family and friends as story characters, just as professional writers often do. In doing this, the children are encouraged to be analytical about their own personalities and to think about how they are perceived by others.

The project uses writing partners and, where suitable, well-known adults to offer support in brainstorming incidents, choosing a suitable event and in planning and writing the story. Proformas are provided for evaluation of the publication by an adult.

Children enjoy writing about their own experiences and begin learning to tell and write personal news stories from a very early age. It is a small but significant step to ask them to use these narratives as the basis for imaginative stories. Some children find it difficult not to assume knowledge on the part of the reader and to select the details that will make these stories comprehensible and interesting.

Through this context, children use a ready-made plot and the challenge is to concentrate on crafting the story well. They should be encouraged to embellish the plot with atmospheric detail and to use the reactions and opinions of other characters to give the story an authentic ring.

This writing project is good for encouraging children to celebrate their writing with others. Those adults who recognise the main event will often show a heightened interest and enjoyment in reading the child's work. Moreover, children are encouraged by this project to live in the world as writers; observing and listening to those around them and recognising the everyday events that often make good material for stories.

Project organisation

At the beginning of the project, children work individually and, if possible, with those at home, to brainstorm events from their own lives that would make good stories. In pairs, they help each other to clarify their story ideas and choose the best. Then, individually, they write a character study of themselves. Supported by a photocopiable sheet, they plot out their stories as a sequenced list of events, deciding whether, where and how to embellish the storyline.

Publication and presentation

The prologue and story are published together on a large sheet of card, along with, if possible, a photograph of the child or main character, at the age they were when the story happened. The size of card will depend on the length of the story, but the layout must leave room for a border, a large story heading and the author's name.

Books the children may find useful

The Goalkeeper's Revenge and Other Stories by Bill Naughton (Penguin)
Boy: An Autobiographical Account by Roald Dahl (Cape)

THE INCIDENT

✝ ⏱ 30

Teaching content
- Brainstorming story ideas from personal experience.
- Selecting possible ideas for development.

What you need
Photocopiable page 116, writing materials.

What to do
Explain that many writers base their stories on personal experience. For instance, Bernard Ashley, who is a primary headteacher, often writes school stories. Use *Dinner Ladies Don't Count* as an example. Tell the children that they are going to write a story based on personal experience. Give each child a copy of photocopiable page 116 and ask them to fill in as many boxes as possible. Emphasise that the incidents can be anything that happened at any time within their living memory; it is okay for children to write about incidents that happened when they were three or four years old, as long as they can remember pertinent details.

If appropriate, you could suggest that the children take their sheets home to ask whether their parents can add any ideas, or remind them of incidents long forgotten. In any case, ask all the children to think about their sheets overnight and to choose two or three good incidents that would form the basis of an interesting story for others to read.

CHOOSING A STORY

✝✝ ⏱ 30

Teaching content
Identifying what makes a good story.

What you need
2–3 incidents identified from the previous activity.

What to do
Put the children into pairs and ask them to tell each other about the two or three incidents they have identified. Partners should help each other to choose the one incident that will make the best basis for a story. Emphasise that storytellers should listen to their partner's advice but that the final decision is theirs and theirs alone.

MY VERY OWN CHARACTER

†† ⏱30

Teaching content
- Using self as a character.
- Writing a character study.

What you need
Photocopiable pages 117 and 118, writing materials.

What to do
Remind the children that the main character in this story is going to be themselves. It is therefore important to draw up a character portrait. Tell the children to work in their pairs and to use photocopiable page 117 to identify

their three or four main personality qualities and how these are shown. The children may find the input of their writing partner useful to offer an objective view of their character.

Show the children the exemplar material on photocopiable page 118. This provides some good examples of how other children chose to write up their character study. Tell the children to write up their character study into a paragraph which will form a prologue to the story. Some children may have chosen qualities that lead directly into the adventure, and if so, they should use this as a link into the main story, as in extract (a). Other children may not and if this is the case, they should round off their character study as in extract (b). In either case, the prologue should fill approximately half a sheet of A4 paper.

PLANNING THE STORY

† ⏱45

Teaching content
- Sequencing and planning the storyline.
- Dividing the story into parts.

What you need
Photocopiable page 119, writing materials.

What to do
Give each child a copy of photocopiable page 119 which asks them to list the main events of their story in chronological order, then to number them so that the chronology is absolutely clear. This list should then help the children to structure their stories. The children are then asked to make notes on the following points:
- Describe the day
- Describe the place
- Describe who was there
- Describe what happened
- Describe how other people reacted – what did they say/do?
- Did this event change the main character in any way?
- Did this event change how others viewed the main character?

These points will help children to elaborate on the events in their lists. Explain that it is this development and elaboration that infuses a

story with life and colour. A mere list of events could be as boring to read as a shopping list.

Now ask the children to use their list of events and the prompts on the photocopiable page to draft their story with a definite beginning, middle and end.

5

WRITING AND PRESENTATION
✝ 60

Teaching content
Redrafting and final presentation.

What you need
Writing materials, pieces of coloured card (at least A3 size), photograph of each child at the age they are in the story, prologues, glue.

What to do
Tell the children to write up their story from their first draft on sheets of A4 paper, writing on one side only. Then give each child a large sheet of card and tell them to write the title in large letters at the top of the left-hand side. They should then stick in the prologue and a photograph of themselves taken at the age they were when the incident took place. The final version of the story should be stuck on the right hand side. If the story runs on to more that one page, the pages can be pasted across the top, one on top of the other as in the illustration, so that the pages turn like a flip-chart.

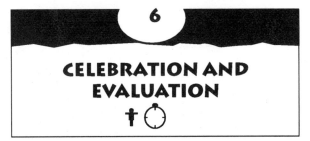

6

CELEBRATION AND EVALUATION
✝ ⏱

Teaching content
Stories are evaluated and reviewed by two different reviewers.

What you need
Completed 'True story' publications, photocopiable page 120, writing materials, glue.

What to do
Completed publications should be taken home and read to an adult who knows the child well. It is preferable if the incident in the story is one that the adult knows about, although this is not essential. If there are problems with the children taking the publication home, then perhaps a suitably friendly adult in the school would be prepared to listen and discuss the story events with the child. The adults should be requested to fill in the evaluation sheet provided on photocopiable page 120. These may be shared with small groups in the class and then stuck on to the back of the card as a special type of review. Writing partners may also like to review stories and these can also be stuck on to the back of the card below the adult's evaluation.

THE INCIDENT

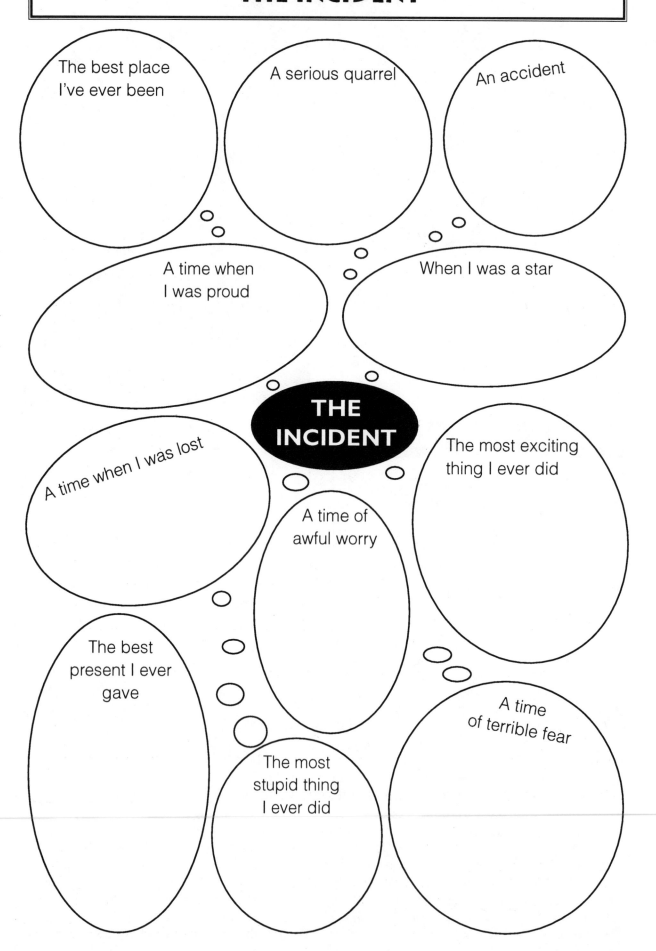

The best place
I've ever been

A serious quarrel

An accident

A time when
I was proud

When I was a star

A time when I was lost

THE
INCIDENT

The most exciting
thing I ever did

A time of
awful worry

The best
present I ever
gave

A time
of terrible fear

The most
stupid thing
I ever did

NAME

MY VERY OWN CHARACTER

◆ Circle the three or four qualities that are central to your character.

sporty   proud   clever

talented in some way   lazy

dreamy   untidy   argumentative

organised   fun-loving   hardworking

funny   kind

other...   other...   other...

How these qualities are shown in my life by:

The things I do _____

_____

The things I say _____

_____

The way I look _____

_____

The things my parent says about me _____

_____

The things my friends say about me_____

_____

MY VERY OWN CHARACTER

Extract (a)

Andrew Smith was a boy of eight. He had blue eyes and blond hair. He was a great animal lover and one of the world's biggest daredevils. His parents said that if he didn't stop talking about animals he would turn into one. Andrew loved animals so much that when the chance arose to look after three baby rabbits, he jumped at it...

Extract (b)

Laura Howarth was a rosy-cheeked girl with long brown hair and bright sparkling eyes. She was a kind, happy girl who loved animals. Her friends said that she was a kind friend to have and her parents said that she was very kind too. It was a few days after Laura's eighth birthday when her most terrible moment of fear occurred.

Scholastic
IMAGINATIVE WRITING
Workshop

PLANNING THE STORY

◆ List the main events in your story in the order in which they happen, then number them.

◆ Then describe the following to help you to elaborate on the main events.

the day:

the place:

who was there...

what happened...

how other people reacted...

Did this event change the main character at all? How? _____

_____

Did this event change how others viewed the main character? How? _____

_____

TRUE STORY – EVALUATION

◆ Please make a brief comment about each of these questions.

1. When you read the prologue did you recognise the character described? Which aspects were particularly recognisable? Were there any that were not recognisable?

2. Please make one positive statement about the character that could be added to the character portrait.

3. Did you know about, or do you remember the incident described in the story? Does it surprise you in any way?

4. Are you surprised that this incident was so important to this child?

5. Do you like the way in which the story begins and ends? Would you prefer a different beginning or ending?

6. Which part of the story do you think is particularly well written?

7. Would you like to read another personal story by this author?

8. Do you know of any other exciting event from the life of this author that you think would make a good story? What is it?

Scholastic
IMAGINATIVE WRITING
Workshop

Chapter Eleven

ADVENTURE AT SEABAY SCHOOL

INTRODUCTION

Project description

In this writing project the children are asked to write a choice adventure story set in a context which should be very familiar to them – that of a school.

Seabay School, the most wonderful school in the world, is threatened with closure. The children are presented with the publisher's book blurb, which gives a brief summary of how the story begins and ends, but leaves open the nature and detail of both the characters and the adventure. Children work in groups of four to create the four characters who eventually save the school, and then in pairs to devise two parallel storylines that end with each child individually describing how the school is saved.

The story is written in the tradition of a school adventure; although the story may be far-fetched, it should remain in the realms of the possible and the temptation to move into magic must be avoided.

Why this context?

Children are familiar with school stories in a variety of genres – from *The Beano*'s 'Bash Street Kids', through Enid Blyton's *Mallory Towers* to Gene Kemp's *The Turbulent Term of Tyke Tyler* and Bernard Ashley's *Dinner Ladies Don't Count* (which is included in this workshop).

Writing in a group ensures that there is a wide range of ideas and, because several writers are working together on the one publication, a complex storyline may be developed in a short time. The project structure is tight enough to ensure that the written work of individuals will dovetail into a single, coherent choice adventure publication. The project raises children's awareness of the choices that may be made within a storyline and gives them the opportunity to plan and write a number of turning points, rather than having to follow only one good idea.

When children work together at the beginning of the project, the shared expertise of four reader-writers ensures lively debate and writing of the highest quality. The children are encouraged to sustain consistent character action and dialogue throughout the story. They are shown how to use structural mechanisms such as cliff-hangers to maintain the reader's interest. The final part of the project challenges them each to write a satisfying ending that resolves all the issues.

Project organisation

The project can be divided into three stages. The first stage of the story is written by children working in groups of four. They support each other in the thinking and writing process to establish characters and generate starting points for the story. The choice adventure is introduced at the second stage, in which children work in pairs to write what happens next. Finally, each child writes his or her own conclusion.

Children write at different rates and the final activities, linked to publishing and presenting the story, ensure that all the children are involved right up to the end of the project. Joint decisions about presentation (border designs, illustrations, illuminated letters and chapter headings) must be made when the first chapter is ready to be stuck into the book. The layout and design of each chapter must be agreed by the whole group before it is stuck into place. It is important that each group works as a team on this project because if any part of this publication is not stuck in its logical place, then the story will be impossible to follow.

A writing group photograph should be organised at the beginning of the project, to be stuck into the back of the book with the authors' biographical details.

Publication and presentation

The story is published using an adapted and customised exercise book or jotter. The structure of a choice adventure is complex and it is advisable for children to follow instructions exactly as they are explained for each task.

You may like to photocopy the group photograph together with the authors' biographical details. These can then be included on any advertising posters and leaflets.

Books the children may find useful

Red Spectacle's Gang by Gordon Snell (Hutchinson)

Siege of Cobb Street School by Hazel Townson (Anderson)

The Turbulent Term of Tyke Tiler by Gene Kemp (Penguin)

The Secret of Weeping Wood by Robert Swindells (Scholastic)

Dinner Ladies Don't Count by Bernard Ashley (Penguin)

POTENTIAL HEROES OF SEABAY SCHOOL

Teaching content
- Making collaborative decisions.
- Creating a balanced set of characters.

What you need

Photocopiable pages 127 and 128, A3-sized paper, writing and drawing materials, glue, jotters.

What to do

Organise the class into groups of four children of mixed ability and explain that they are going to plan and write a book together. Sometimes they will be writing individually, sometimes in pairs and sometimes in groups of four.

Give each group a copy of the book blurb on photocopiable page 127. Tell them that this is the back cover blurb for the book that they are about to write. Discuss the information the blurb gives us about this story and tell the children that their first task is to create the characters of the four children who look after the library at Seabay School.

Ask the children to suggest examples of school adventure stories and write these on the board. Then discuss the types of characters that are found in typical school adventure stories. Children may point out that characters are often:
- of different genders;
- of slightly different ages;
- of different types of personality;
- perhaps of different ethnic origins.

Give each group a copy of photocopiable page 128 and a large sheet of paper folded into four sections, one for each character. Tell them that they must create the characters for their group story. Point out that certain talents and abilities may prove useful in their forthcoming adventures. For example, understanding a language other than English, having a sympathy with animals or being a competent sailor or climber may save the group from danger. Remind the children that the unfolding storyline belongs to them.

When they come to deciding personality, suggest that groups consider the characteristics on the bottom of photocopiable page 128.

Tell the children to be sure that they have a well-balanced group of characters. Give them 15–20 minutes to make notes in the four sections of the paper. Then ask one child from each group to report on one of their characters and invite comment on the credibility of the character study from the rest of the class.

Give each group a blank jotter and four sheets of paper to fit inside it. Ask each child to write one character study and to sketch a portrait to accompany it. Stick these into the front pages of the book, leaving the first three pages blank for title page, dedication and contents. Stick one copy of the blurb from photocopiable page 127 on to the back cover of the book. Explain that the first three pages (title page, dedication and contents) will be completed after the story is written.

IN THE LIBRARY

Teaching content
- Writing dialogue.
- Writing a first sentence.

What you need

Photocopiable page 127, A3-sized paper, writing materials.

What to do

Ask the children to re-read the book blurb on photocopiable page 127 so that they are reminded of the bare bones of this story. Tell the children that the opening scene will take place in the school library. The characters are in the library, discussing the problems of the building repairs.

Give each group a sheet of A3 paper divided into four and ask them to write the name of one character in each portion. Ask them to discuss and note down what each character is doing as the story opens. Remind the children that whatever each character is doing must be consistent with their personality description from the previous activity.

Next, children must decide and write in a speech bubble what each character is saying about the school. Again, their words must be in character. Lastly, as a group, a good first sentence must be devised for Chapter One.

Children should craft the first sentence and the information about what the characters are doing and saying into a first paragraph, which should be scribed in rough by one person, with alterations and editing being suggested by the whole group. This rough copy should be saved and copied out after the next activity.

THE SECRET PLACE

Teaching content
Developing end-of-chapter cliff-hangers.

What you need
Writing and illustration materials, scissors, glue, jotters.

What to do
Explain that the children must now decide how their characters find the hidden room, cave or cellar in the library. If you are certain that all will contribute, ask the children simply to discuss and reach a decision about how the room was found. If there are concerns that some children may not contribute, ask each child to write down an idea and tell the group to discuss each idea in turn before deciding on one.

Ask the children to re-read the first part of Chapter One which they wrote in the previous activity. They should then work together to continue the story up to the moment when the hidden room is discovered. Explain that the chapter should end on a cliff-hanger with the characters staring in amazement into the hidden place. You will probably find that children have a good understanding of cliff-hangers from watching television serials; they know that each episode must end at an exciting point to maintain the viewer's interest.

Tell two children to write up this first chapter, dividing the writing between them, and two children to illustrate the chapter, inserting the pictures where appropriate. Children must be responsible for cutting paper to size for each task and sticking them into the jotter under the heading Chapter One, and an appropriate chapter title if they so desire.

Tell them they must leave room at the bottom of the last page of Chapter One to write in the first 'choice' instructions.

THE FIND!

Teaching content
- Creating alternative storylines.
- Describing place.
- Writing dialogue.

What you need
Photocopiable page 129, writing and illustration materials, jotters, glue.

What to do
Explain that the children are writing a 'choice' book, which means that they must write alternative storylines so that the reader can choose what happens next in the story. Have any of them read books like these? Discuss how they work. Tell the children that the first choice in their adventure will be made at the end of Chapter 1. Sub-divide the groups into writing pairs, and explain that pairs must decide what is found in the secret room. Give each pair a copy of photocopiable page 129 which may help to generate ideas. Ask each pair to choose an idea, and then tell them to check that they have chosen a different idea from the other pair in their group. If both pairs have chosen the same idea, one pair must give it up and choose again.

Explain that Chapter One will end with 'When the children entered the secret place, if you think they found A, then turn to page X, if you think they found B, then turn to page XX'. The children should insert their chosen ideas instead of A and B. The page numbers will be filled in later. In this way, the reader can decide which storyline to follow.

Next, writing pairs should plan Chapter Two together, beginning with a description of the secret room/place found by the characters. Remind the children of the importance of atmospheric writing and ask them to write a paragraph about this place. Next, tell the children to write collaboratively about what is found in the room and include a discussion among the characters about the significance of their find. Remind them that the dialogue must be a true reflection of character. The rough draft should be a collaborative piece of writing, thought through and then edited by both. Finally, tell each pair to swap their rough draft with the

other pair in their group and to check each other's stories for inconsistencies, editing them where necessary.

Writing pairs should then write out and illustrate Chapter Two. When complete, the group should lay out the writing and illustrations and stick both Chapter Twos into the adventure book, beginning each on a new page. Remind the children to leave room at the end of these chapters to write in the next choice.

HOW THEY SAVED THE SCHOOL

Teaching content

- Turning points.
- Endings.

What you need

Photocopiable page 129, writing and illustration materials, jotters, glue.

What to do

Explain that the turning point and ending to the story will now be decided and written individually, so that there will be four alternative Chapter Threes for the reader to choose from.

Each Chapter Two will end with the following list of choices:

If you think **A** happens, turn to page X
If you think **B** happens, turn to page XX
If you think **C** happens, turn to page XXX
If you think **D** happens, turn to page XXXX

Of course, this means that all four of these options must be consistent with both of the Chapter Twos. This is quite complicated and the children may find it too restricting. An easier alternative is to offer two options at the end of the first Chapter Two and two more at the end of the second.

Give each child a copy of photocopiable page 129 which suggests some turning points, some of which may be appropriate to the storylines which children have developed so far, but stress that the children may follow their own ideas if they prefer. Before writing, the children must check that they have chosen different routes for the storyline to develop, or readers will not have a choice.

Now individuals should write the middle and ending to the adventure story. Remind them that they must tie up all the loose ends and that the characters in the book save their school from being closed down. The story could end with a school celebration to thank the intrepid adventurers.

Ask the children to swap their work with others in their group and to read and edit each other's stories for sense, coherence, style, punctuation and spelling. They should then write out their edited chapter and illustrate it appropriately, sticking it in the jotter following the Chapter Twos.

The group should then check through the whole book filling in the missing page numbers in the choice statements and checking that the cross-references match.

Using activities from the presentation chapter as guidance, ask the children to divide the work involved in writing, designing and illustrating the cover, title page, dedication and contents list for the blank pages at the front of the book.

EVALUATING THE CHOICE ADVENTURE

✝ ⏱(40)

Teaching content

Writing positive, concise evaluations.

What you need

Choice adventure stories, chalkboard, self-adhesive labels (such as Post-it notes), writing materials.

What to do

Ask the groups to swap their stories so that every child can write an evaluation of someone else's book. Before they read the adventures, ask the children to consider the following points, grading them where necessary (A excellent; B good; C average; D poor; O awful):
• Presentation
• General storyline
• Who was the most interesting character?
• Which is the best illustration?
• What is the best part of the story?
• One excellent point about the book
• One piece of advice for the authors in preparation for their next publication
Write these on the board so that children can refer to them.

Discuss how important it is for feedback to be positive and constructive, as negative responses can hurt and are not helpful, particularly when publication is complete. Comments should be honest, but there is always something good to be found in another's work. Tell the children that their comments will be written on a self-adhesive label so they must be very concise.

Now give the children plenty of time to read the publication, following several of the choices on offer, before writing their evaluation on a self-adhesive label. After writing, the notes should be stuck on the back of the books which should be returned to the authors to be read and considered.

A good finishing point for this activity is to invite every child to read out one point from all the evaluations on their book that they find particularly useful.

REVIEWS

✝ ⏱(40)

Teaching content

Writing a punchy review.

What you need

Choice adventure stories, photocopiable page 130, writing materials.

What to do

Tell the children that many books have quotations from reviews on their back covers. Show the children any examples of these that you can find in the classroom and explain that they are intended to encourage readers to dip into the book.

Give each child a copy of photocopiable page130 so that they can see how this exercise has been carried out by children in another school. Tell the children that they are going to take one of the evaluations of their book from the previous activity, and take the most positive words, phrases and sentences to produce a couple of review sentences to write on the back cover of their adventure books. Each child in the group should then write the review on to the back cover under the book blurb. Reviews should be written in quotation marks and the reviewer's name written underneath.

POTENTIAL HEROES OF SEABAY SCHOOL

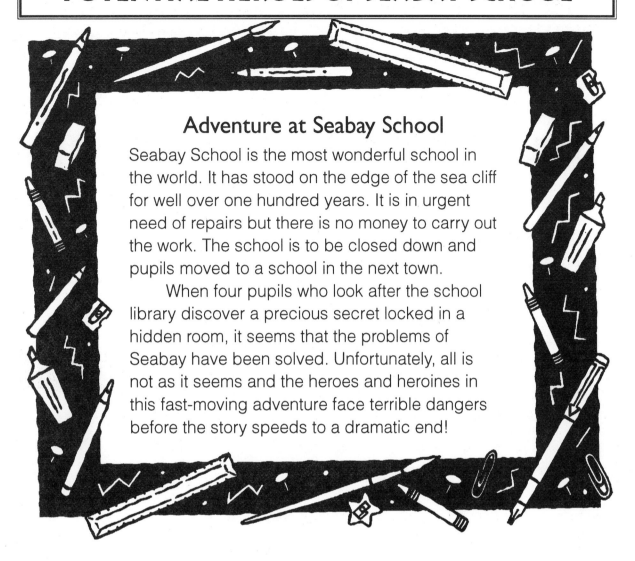

Adventure at Seabay School

Seabay School is the most wonderful school in the world. It has stood on the edge of the sea cliff for well over one hundred years. It is in urgent need of repairs but there is no money to carry out the work. The school is to be closed down and pupils moved to a school in the next town.

When four pupils who look after the school library discover a precious secret locked in a hidden room, it seems that the problems of Seabay have been solved. Unfortunately, all is not as it seems and the heroes and heroines in this fast-moving adventure face terrible dangers before the story speeds to a dramatic end!

Reviews

POTENTIAL HEROES OF SEABAY SCHOOL

◆ As a group, decide the following about the four characters.

1. What gender are the four characters?

2. What ethnic origin are the four characters?

3. What is each character called?

4. What age are the four characters?

5. What is the main personality trait (see below) of each character?

6. What do they look like?

7. What special talents do they have?

8. What hobbies do they enjoy?

◆ When considering character, look at some of these qualities and decide which might belong to the four. Some qualities may of course belong to every character. Be careful not to have contradictory qualities for the same character.

dreamy   argumentative   aggressive

kind   hardworking

helpful   determined   daring

noisy   funny   brave   timid

fun-loving   clever   secretive

sporty   organised   lazy   shy   quiet

THE FIND!

What do the children find?

An old painting
A gang hideout
A map
A treasure chest

A tunnel leading underground to...
A coded message saying...
A bin-bag full of new banknotes

Possible turning points

A boat is paddled into the cave.

The gang return and find the children.

The school bully sees the coded message and...

The secret door closes trapping the children in the soundproof hidden room.

The map directs the children to an island surrounded by dangerous seas.

The canvas rips and behind the picture is...

The children hear the gang planning the next raid.

REVIEWS

◆ These are copies of real reviews written by children about choice adventure books.

Presentation: A
Storyline: A
Best picture: on page 14
Best part of the story: 'Hey look! The jewels are floating
out of my pocket!'
One excellent point about the book: The pictures are very good.
One piece of advice: Keep the good work up.

" 'The jewels are floating out of my pocket!'
These were the words that carried forward this excellent book.
Illustrations are excellent. This book is a must for all lovers of
choice adventure stories."

Presentation: A
Storyline: A, but it was a bit hard to understand Chapter 2 part 1.
Best picture: the Egyptian tombs
Best part of the story: page 3–4
One excellent point about the book: illustrations
One piece of advice: Make sure the story is clear.

" A beautifully-illustrated and presented book. Difficult in parts, but
I give it an A. Don't miss this new publication Secrets of the Ruby
Key."

Scholastic WRITING Workshop

Chapter Twelve

THE BULLY

INTRODUCTION

Project description

In this project the children work with a writing partner to write a story about bullying. This is presented in the form of a flip-over book in which the same story is told from two viewpoints: that of the bully and that of the victim. The victim's story is told from the front of the book to the middle, the book is then flipped over, so that its back becomes the new front cover. The bully's story is told from this point to the middle. The stories meet in the centre of the book with a bird's-eye view of a meeting of the two main characters, forming a joint ending.

The children begin the project by choosing a club or organisation to which the two main characters belong. Together they create both characters and write short descriptions of them. These character descriptions form a prologue to each story. Partners then decide on the specific event that gives the bully an opportunity to challenge the victim. They each write this up as a chapter, one told from the viewpoint of the bully, the other told through the eyes of the victim. Then the two children invent a situation that forces a twist in the story and changes the relationship between the two characters. The story ends on the centre pages which show the characters shaking hands and resolving their differences. It is suggested that the children write one chapter from each viewpoint.

Why this context?

This project provides an opportunity for children to explore two characters' viewpoints within one story. It highlights the possible effects of an author's decision to tell the story through the eyes of one of the characters, and the powerful effect this can have. Each story is written in the first person and, if the children write one chapter from each viewpoint, they learn to develop characterisation by adopting very different speech styles, actions and thoughts, writing in this very direct style. Children long to see bullies defeated and victims triumph and this motivates them, ensuring an emotionally satisfying experience as well as inventive twists in the storyline.

The flip-over is an interesting publishing format which provides good opportunities for children to discuss layout and illustration issues.

The format fascinates both adult and child readers, encouraging them to spend time exploring the book and reading the story. Such avid audience appreciation underlines the pleasure to be gained from writing books that are read and truly enjoyed.

Project organisation

Children work with writing partners to plan the opening of this book and invent the two main characters, but write the character descriptions individually. They read and comment on each other's work and plan the chapter events as a pair before once again writing the two chapters detailing the bully's and victim's stories individually. They return to plan final chapter events together, before once again writing them separately.

It would be helpful if children have first read *Nice/Nasty Neighbours* included in this workshop, and have carried out the structure activities based on that book.

Publication and presentation

The book is published as an A4-sized flip-over book. It can be made from four pieces of A3 cartridge or sugar paper that have been folded and sewn or stapled in the middle so that each book contains eight leaves in all. Prologues giving the character description should be stuck on the first right-hand page of each story, along with an illustration of the character. The stories should be written and illustrated on separate pieces of paper and stuck on to the book pages as each chapter is finished. A double-page spread is allowed for each chapter. It is advisable for each pair of children to lay out each chapter and organise the writing, along with the position and size of illustrations, completely before sticking the pieces into place.

Books the children may find useful

Willy the Champ by Anthony Browne (J. MacRae Books)
Willy the Wimp by Anthony Browne (J. MacRae Books)
Trouble with the Tucker Twins by Rose Impey (Viking)
Hector the Bully by Dinah Priestly (Dent)
All My Men by Bernard Ashley (Penguin)
Sink or Swim by Ghillian Potts (Young Corgi)
Tom Takes Tea/Tom The Hero by Althea Braithwaite and Rob McCaig (Pan Macmillan)
Clever Clive by Joan Lingard (Pan Macmillan)
Hook, Line and Stinker by Robin Kingsland (Pan Macmillan)

PUTTING IT INTO CONTEXT

🕴🕴 ⏱60

Teaching content
Establishing the context.

What you need
Art materials.

What to do
Arrange the class in pairs. Explain to the children that they will need to plan their storyline based on the following framework.

The story will concern two children who are members of a club or team. One of the characters is a bully and the other is the bully's victim. The story begins with a confrontation between the two. The bully then challenges the other character to a test of some kind that will most certainly be won by the bully. Just as the challenge is about to take place, an incident occurs that changes the relationship between the two characters.

Explain that the children will be writing the events from two points of view: one story will tell the events from the viewpoint of the bully; the other will begin at the other end of the book and tell the story from the point of view of the victim. The middle pages will show a bird's-eye view of the two characters shaking hands in resolution of their differences.

As a first step in the creation of their storyline, ask the children to decide the club or team to which the two characters belong. Suggest that the children choose a club or team that is familiar to them. Ask the children to make a badge or logo for the club. This could be used later as part of the cover design for the book.

CREATING THE CHARACTERS

🕴🕴 ⏱60

Teaching content
Creating strongly contrasting characters.

What you need
Photocopiable pages 138 and 139, writing materials.

What to do
Remind the class that the story is going to be told from two very different viewpoints. The most direct way of indicating a point of view is to write in the first person. To do this, the writer needs to 'step into their character's shoes' and imagine that they are this person. A thorough knowledge of the character is therefore essential.

Give each pair of children a copy of photocopiable pages 138 and 139 and ask them to work together to fill out one sheet for each character. Remind the children that most people are a mixture of good and bad points, but that this story needs strongly contrasting characters. It is a good idea, therefore, to exaggerate good and bad qualities. The children will need to know both characters well to write their stories. This is why both members of each pair should work on both character inventions.

Explain that the children will be using these character sketches in the next writing task.

THE PROLOGUE
Teaching content
Writing in the first person.

What you need
Prepared flip-over book, chalkboard, completed character sheets (photocopiable pages 138 and 139 from previous activity), writing and art materials, glue.

What to do
Explain to the children that each story will be written in the first person, with the characters talking directly to the reader. Each story will begin with a prologue which will be used to introduce the character who is telling the story and to set the scene.

Depending on the experience of the children in the class, you may decide to write up a number of alternative beginnings on the board. For example:

Thought you might like to hear about one of the great adventures in my life. First, let me introduce myself. My name is...

Ever heard of the .... club/team? I'm a member of that team/club and I'm going to tell you about something that happened to me a short time ago. First I'd better introduce myself...

Up until six months ago if you'd asked me what I thought about ... I would have told you he/she was one of my worst enemies, but something happened that changed all that. My name is...

It's funny how friendships are made and how people come to like or dislike one another. ... and I used to hate each other, but now we're sworn friends. My name is...

Explain that there are really two books to be written and writing partners must decide who is to write from each point of view. Once decided, tell children to use the character sketches and to write the prologue to the book.

Once written and corrected, these may be written neatly on to one page and stuck on to the first right-hand page of the prepared book, one at the front and one flipped over on the first right-hand page at the back.

From now on, each consecutive double-page spread will be used to set out each chapter and, if there is space, will be illustrated appropriately.

4

CHAPTER 1: THE CHALLENGE

Teaching content

Looking at the same event from two different points of view.

What you need

Photocopiable page 140, writing and art materials, flip-over book, glue.

What to do

Explain that Chapter 1 will open with some small happening which gives the bully the opportunity to challenge the other character. The event could be as small as an accidental splash in the swimming pool, or an unintentional push on the football pitch. Perhaps the victim stands on the bully's foot by mistake. Children must decide what the incident is and then consider what challenge the bully makes.

Give each pair a copy of photocopiable page 140 ask them to discuss and complete it. Then tell them to select their best idea for the challenge and to decide where the two characters will arrange to meet in order to see the challenge through. If the children will find this difficult, suggest some ideas or brainstorm ideas as a class before allowing partners to complete the sheet.

Having planned the chapter together, writing partners should decide who is to write the next chapter in the story from each viewpoint. They may decide to continue with the characters first

chosen or to swap. Either way, they should re-read the appropriate prologue leading into their chapter before beginning to write. Remind the writers to include some of the phrases from the photocopiable sheet, describing the way in which the characters show their feelings.

Once written, and edited if necessary, these may be copied neatly on to separate paper and stuck into the appropriate double-page spreads of the book, along with any illustrations the children wish to include.

5

CHAPTER 2: THE TWIST

Teaching content

Turning points in a story.

What you need

Writing and art materials, flip-over book, glue.

What to do

Chapter 2 will open with the two characters approaching the meeting place. Writing partners must now decide what the event will be that changes the relationship between the two characters. Suggest some ideas to the children in order to spark off their own ideas:

- intruders may come along causing trouble and forcing the two to join together as a team;
- a younger child or perhaps an animal could be in trouble and the two could 'save the day' together;
- the challenge could put one character (the bully?) into a seriously dangerous situation to be rescued by the other character.

Brainstorm other ideas with the children and ask them to think about a good twist for their own story. If children have difficulty with this, join pairs into groups of four and let each pair tell their story to the other partnership, who should listen carefully and suggest ideas.

Finally, once the twist has been agreed, writing partners should decide who is going to write Chapter 2 from each perspective. The chapter should begin with the thoughts of the characters as they approach the meeting. You may wish to include a stream of consciousness, in which case some of the activities from the characterisation chapter of *Aspects of the Craft of Writing* may be used to plan the writing. Some children may need the help of a starter sentence, such as 'As I walked towards the meeting place I thought...' Then, writers should describe the events of the twist and end with the character admitting his/her changed opinion of the other. Explain that this admission may be a little grudging (it is still early in the new relationship for each to know the other well), but there should be an indication that there is a possibility of permanent friendship and change in the future.

Once written, and edited if possible, the two versions of this chapter may be copied neatly on to separate paper and stuck into the appropriate double-page spreads of the book, along with any illustrations.

THE HANDSHAKE

Teaching content
Writing direct speech.

What you need
Photocopiable page 141, writing and art materials, flip-over book, glue.

What to do
Give each child in the pair a copy of photocopiable page 141 and ask them to decide what each character says as the two shake hands. Continuing the theme of Chapter 2, their words should reflect a promise of future friendship as this is the resolution to the story.

The children should decide who is to fill in the speech bubble for which character. Each child should fill in the speech bubble on their sheet and then the two of them can be glued into place on the centre page of the flip-over book with hands meeting along the centre line. One picture will be stuck on one way and the second the other way up, giving the impression of two people shaking hands. The children may now draw in details on the centre page in order to elaborate upon the scene. Remind them that this is an aerial view of the world and that they will have to make rough sketches to ensure that all objects are drawn correctly. This is a very difficult, but enjoyable, task. Indoor scenes will include bird's-eye views of furniture, lamps, telephones and so on. Outdoor scenes may include treetops, rooftops, streets, rivers and so on.

The writing partners should decide on a good title for their book and then each should make the cover for one of the starting points. Covers may be drawn directly on to the book or on separate card/paper to be stuck on later. The children could incorporate the logos they created in the first activity. Remind the children about writing the authors' names on both covers and of the other information that is often found on the front cover of a book. If the children need guidance with this, activity 1 in the presentation chapter deals specifically with book covers.

CELEBRATION AND EVALUATION
†† (50)

Teaching content
Writing a book review.

What you need
Completed flip-over books, photocopiable page 142, writing materials.

What to do
Once the flip-over book has been completed, tell each pair that they are going to write a review of their own book. Give each child a copy of photocopiable page 142 which contains questions about the story. The pair should read their story together and then complete the photocopiable page independently.

When they have finished ask them to compare and discuss their answers, and then to use as many of the ideas as they wish to write a joint book review. This should be written in such a way as to persuade others to read their book. The photocopiable review sheets, plus the final review, can form the basis of an interesting display focusing on the review process.

Encourage the children to set up and participate in a special two-week loan scheme so that others may borrow and read their books.

CREATING THE CHARACTERS

Bully

Name:

Age:

Gender:

Physical characteristics:

Height

Build

Colour and style of hair

Preferred style of dress

Other distinguishing traits

Disposition

What makes this person angry?

What makes this person laugh?

What makes this person proud?

What does this person like most in the world?

What does this person hate most in the world?

Give two reasons why this character dislikes the other main character in the story:

1.

2.

Scholastic
IMAGINATIVE WRITING
Workshop

CREATING THE CHARACTERS

Victim

Name:

Age:

Gender:

Physical characteristics:

Height

Build

Colour and style of hair

Preferred style of dress

Other distinguishing traits

Disposition

What makes this person angry?

What makes this person laugh?

What makes this person proud?

What does this person like most in the world?

What does this person hate most in the world?

Give two reasons why this character dislikes the other main character in the story:

1.

2.

CHAPTER 1: THE CHALLENGE

◆ The bully may dare the other character to do something.
What might the dare be?

Dare 1

Dare 2

Perhaps the bully threatens the character. What is the threat?

Threat 1

Threat 2

Maybe the bully suggests a contest to see who is best. What might this be?

Contest 1

Contest 2

◆ Consider all these ideas. Tick the best idea and use this in your story.

◆ Now consider how the characters might be feeling about the challenge and how they would show their feelings. Put B (Bully) or V (Victim) by each word or phrase. Add some of your own if you wish.

weak, trembling knees	triumphant smile
power sick, empty stomach	dry mouth
wide, frightened eyes	confident, straight back
brave smile domineering leer	cruel, narrow eyes

THE HANDSHAKE

CELEBRATION AND EVALUATION

◆ Write *two* statements that identify what makes this a story worth reading.

◆ Select the most powerful sentence from this story. It may be a sentence that makes the reader want to read on, that tantalises the reader, that makes the reader laugh or cry or that simply portrays the place or character perfectly.

◆ Choose one page that you think is particularly well presented in terms of layout and illustration.

◆ Name someone from your class who you think would particularly enjoy reading this story. Why have you chosen them?

◆ Write one sentence that sums up the appeal of this story. Some of the words and phrases from the list below might help you.

totally absorbing	powerful	dramatic	sensitive
satisfying	rich ideas	warm	lively
vividly written	impressive	enchanting	tragic
surprising	closely observed	heart-rending	funny
exciting	gripping	fascinating	serious
emotional	fast-moving	realistic	gritty
thrilling	mysterious	frightening	sad
charming	action-packed	pleasing	witty
pertinent	delightful	true to life	magic

Scholastic
IMAGINATIVE WRITING
Workshop

Scholastic WRITING Workshop

Chapter Thirteen

PRESENTATION

INTRODUCTION

This section details generic activities that could be applied to any of the writing projects in this book or to any piece of writing your pupils do. Whereas the specific projects detail activities that help children to generate and craft a story, the activities in this section suggest ways to involve children in the process of publishing their stories and seeing them read by others.

Publishing is the final stage of the writing process, in which the product is put into a completed format with a cover, illustrations, author biographical details, dedication and/or any other features the author wishes to include. Publication is important because it provides a lasting record of achievement and a reference point for future work. Although it takes time, it is the all-important final step for a young writer – the time when the purpose and the effort come together in an end product that creates delight and emotional satisfaction. Through publication children celebrate their good work and become aware of the work of others, but also witness people reading and enjoying their stories. It is a powerful way to build and harness the children's:

• enthusiasm for writing;
• understanding of audience and audience needs;
• commitment to high standards of work;
• emotional satisfaction in producing high quality work.

Publication also allows the child to review and revisit old pieces of work, providing an invaluable resource for discussion of progress, standards and audience.

Children can learn how to vary the presentation of their stories artistically by being given lots of opportunities to look at, copy and adapt published work. Always encourage them to introduce their own ideas when copying so that part of the work becomes their own personal contribution. They quickly learn to use different styles observed and gradually they blend ideas gleaned from different sources to produce new and original work.

The activities in the first part of this chapter draw children's attention to various book features which they may wish to include in their finished publications. These are followed by activities that offer specific presentation ideas for calligraphy, illuminated letters and borders.

Finally there are some activities that detail ideas for celebrating published work and sharing it with a wider audience.

You will want to refer to this chapter whenever children are nearing completion and publication of their stories. The activities can be used as one-off lessons to raise children's awareness of specific aspects of publishing, or incorporated into a mini-topic in which children set up and run a classroom-based publishing enterprise to raise their awareness of the world of work as well as specific aspects of publishing.

Creating a publishing centre

If possible, try to set up an area where resources for publishing are readily available. The following is a suggested (but by no means exhaustive) list of items that could be included:
• pencils and pens in various colours
• lined and plain paper in various sizes
• pencil sharpeners
• erasers
• calligraphy pens and ink
• coloured paper
• crayons
• painting equipment
• scissors

- glue
- needles and thread
- stapler and staples
- word processor
- wallpaper samples
- scraps of fabric
- wool
- hole punch
- adhesive tape
- rulers
- string
- ribbon
- old greeting cards/photographs/catalogues
- stencils
- sequins
- tissue paper
- coloured cellophane.

Useful books

The following is a list of books that you may find helpful for finding ideas about making and publishing books:

A Book of One's Own by Paul Johnson (Hodder and Stoughton)

Bright Ideas Writing and Making Books by Moira Andrew (Scholastic)

How a Book is Made (Puffin Resource Pack, Penguin)

How to be Brilliant at Making Books by I. Yates (Brilliant Publications)

Making a Book by Mandy Suhr (Wayland)

Making a Book by Ruth Thomson (Franklin Watts)

1

THE COVER STORY

Teaching content

Developing knowledge about book features (cover).

What you need

A selection of published illustrated books with various styles of cover design, chalkboard, writing and drawing materials, photocopiable page 156, for each child a story they have recently written and want to publish.

What to do

The cover is an extremely important part of a book. It provides essential information about the story and acts as an exciting invitation to tempt the reader to pick the book up off the shelf and read it.

Give the class a couple of minutes to look at the selection of books, but tell them not to open them. Then ask the children which book they would most like to open and why. List the various reasons suggested on the board. If you have time, ask the children if they think that all age groups/sections of society would be attracted by similar things: what about younger children? toddlers? adults? old people? males? females?... List children's suggestions for these under subheadings on the board. If you feel that children are producing rather stereotypical suggestions, you can suggest later that they conduct an investigation to see if those features they have identified are truly significant.

Now, put the children into pairs. Ask them to study the book covers again and, this time, to list the features and essential information on them. These will generally include:

- the book title
- author's name
- illustrator's name
- publisher
- publisher's logo
- back cover 'blurb'
- review quotes
- price
- ISBN (International Standard Book Number).

Then give each pair a copy of photocopiable page 156. Ask them to choose a book and fill in the sheet using the information given on their book cover. Make sure all the children understand the terms on the sheet – for example that a 'blurb' is the publisher's description of the book, that a 'logo' is a symbol or emblem, that the ISBN is the international standard book number used for ordering and identification purposes.

Finally, ask the children to produce individually a rough draft of a book cover for a story they have written. In doing this, they should consider how to lay out all the essential information, working out any problems with the position, style and size of letters, and they should consider the style and size of illustration that is most appropriate for the story and intended readership. Some children may like to do this using a computer if a suitable graphics package is available.

On a practical note, you may like to suggest that the children draw borders around the edge of their cover and you may like to do a lettering lesson with your class (see activity 10).

THE PUBLISHER'S LOGOS

⊛-†† ③⓪

Teaching content

Developing knowledge about book features.

What you need

A selection of published books by various publishers (you can use the books provided in the workshop), writing and drawing materials.

What to do

Explain that every book is published by a publisher and that usually the publisher has its name and/or logo somewhere on the cover. The purpose of the publishing logo is to provide a quick, clear way in which the reader can identify who published the book. Take one book as an example and identify the publisher's logo clearly for the children.

Put the children into pairs and tell them that they have 10 minutes to find, write and draw as many different publishers and their logos as possible.

Then, with the class, briefly go through all those that were found. If you wish, allocate one publisher and logo per pair and ask them to reproduce it on a poster-sized sheet of paper for display.

Encourage the children to consider the variety of publisher's logos. Suggest that they invent a name for their own publishing company and design an appropriate logo for it. These can be displayed with the other publishers' logos above, and children can use their own logos on books they produce.

THE PUBLISHER'S BLURB

†‡† ⑥⓪

Teaching content

- Writing functional text.
- Responding to texts.

What you need

A selection of published books (including those supplied in the workshop) with a publisher's 'blurb' on them, stories that the children have written/published, writing materials, photocopiable page 157 (optional).

What to do

The purpose of this activity is to give children an opportunity to examine publishers' blurbs on books in order to give them varied and useful models to follow when writing about each other's books. Children will get the 'feel' of how to reproduce this style of writing through reading and talking about how blurb-writing differs from story-writing.

Give the children time to examine the selection of books with examples of publishers' blurbs on the back or the inside cover. Ask them to read a few and think about how this writing differs from story-writing:

- What is its purpose?
- Who might read it, and why?
- What sort of comments are made about the books?
- What sort of words and language are used?
- What is the best length for this sort of work?

Now ask the children to work with a partner. Explain that they are each going to write a blurb to promote their partner's book. Tell them to swap stories and to read their partner's work twice: the first time just to enjoy the story, but the second time to find a couple of exciting sentences from any part of the story. These must be sentences that would make a reader want to read this story in full. They should be recorded on photocopiable page 157 as 'quotable quotes'.

The children should then begin their blurb with these quotable quotes, followed by a few sentences recommending their partner's book to others, stating what makes the book a 'good read'. Finally, they should end with a punchy statement about the sort of book this is and the type of person who would enjoy it.

If there is room, the blurb could be stuck on to the back or inside front cover of the book when it is published. If there is no space anywhere on the book itself, the blurb could be displayed on the wall, or incorporated into publicity posters as part of a book launch (see activity 15, page 154).

4

BEYOND THE COVER

Teaching content
Developing knowledge of how books are organised and internal book features.

What you need
A selection of illustrated published books (including those provided in the workshop), chalkboard, photocopiable page 158, writing materials, photocopiable page 159.

What to do
The purpose of this activity is to draw children's attention to the internal features of books and how they are organised. The publications in your selection will obviously vary in detail, but there are a number of basic internal features

that children should be aware of in order to make informed choices for their own publications.

Give the class a couple of minutes to look at the selection of books. Ask them to look at the first few pages of the book (before the story or main text starts) and the last few pages (after the story or main text ends). What do they find on these pages?

Then bring the children together and in discussion with them, make a class list on the board of some common features. These might include:

- title page
- publishing information (publisher's address, year of publication, copyright details)
- dedication
- author details
- list of books by the same author
- list of books in the same series
- contents
- index
- acknowledgements.

Ask the children to work with a partner and give each pair a copy of photocopiable page 158. Let them choose a book from the selection you have provided, or one of their own choice, and complete the photocopiable sheet using the information they find.

A selection of publishing graphics for children to use in their own publications is provided on photocopiable page 159.

DEDICATIONS

w→† 20

Teaching content

Developing awareness about how and why authors write dedications.

What you need

A selection of published books containing dedications.

What to do

Show the children the selection of books and ask them to leaf through the first few pages of each book to find the dedication. Where are they usually found? Discuss with the children how writers sometimes dedicate their books to people they remember and write about in their stories; sometimes the dedication is to a person who has inspired their writing; occasionally books are dedicated to people who are not actually in the story but who are loved and admired by the author. It is a great honour to have a book dedicated to you.

The children should make a note of any dedications they particularly like and use them as a model when writing their own.

ABOUT THE AUTHOR

††→w→† 30

Teaching content

- Developing awareness of book features.
- Personal writing.

What you need

Writing materials, a selection of published books (including those provided in the workshop) some with author's biographical details and some without, chalkboard, photocopiable page 160.

What to do

Show the children the books and ask whether anyone ever reads the author's biographical details. Give the children time to examine the books, asking them to look specifically for information about the author. Have the children noticed whether *all* books have this type of information? What sort of books do/don't?

In pairs, ask the children to look at the books in more detail and this time to read the author biographies. Ask them to construct as full a list as they can of the types of information mentioned. Allow about 20 minutes for this.

Have a quick class brainstorm of the results. As the children report their findings, write them on the board in question form. You should end up with quite a long list of questions, such as:
- What is the name of the author?
- Where does the author live?
- How did the author begin writing?
- What are the author's interests and hobbies?
- For how many years has the author been writing?
- Has the author got any previous publications?
- What does the author enjoy about writing?
- Does the author intend to write any more books?
- What is the author's background and family situation?
- What is the author's age?
- Does the author have any other achievements?

Tell the children that they are going to write an author's biography for themselves. Each child should select the five most interesting/ essential questions and write these and the answers on photocopiable page 160. The completed page should then be used as the basis for an 'About the author' paragraph.

Once finished, the work should be read to writing partners, who should comment on whether it constitutes a reasonable summary of the person concerned.

It may be useful to store this particular piece of writing on a word processor, giving each child two print-outs - one for the book they are currently writing, and one to glue inside their writing/drafting jotters for future reference. As children write and publish more books, they can update, change and adapt what they have written about themselves.

When children use the 'About the author' work on their published books, it is fun to add a small photograph or picture of the author.

7
ORGANISATION OF STORY BOOKS
✝✝ ⏱30

Teaching content

Developing knowledge about book organisation and genre.

What you need

A selection of fiction books by various publishers for different ages, in a variety of genres, writing materials, a book about to be published.

What to do

Explain that story books can be organised in various ways. Some books are divided into chapters, others are not. Of those books with chapters, some list chapter titles/headings at the front of the book on a contents page, others simply number the chapters or write the chapter heading/title at the top of the page, making no reference to this elsewhere in the book.

Ask each pair to find one example of each type of story book organisation:
• a book not divided into chapters;
• a book divided into chapters with a contents page at the front;
• a book divided into chapters, but with no contents page.

Emphasise that it *must* be a fiction book for this activity – information books have a different set of 'rules' and options.

Ask the children to hold up the books they have found that are not divided into chapters. Do they share any common characteristics in terms of:
• the likely readership (age? sex? interests?);
• the type of story (genre – fairy tales, comic strip, etc.);
• the balance between illustrations and text.

Now do the same for those books with chapters and contents pages, and for those with chapters but no contents page.

End by telling the class that when they think about publishing their own books, they must think about these issues and choose the organisation that would be most appropriate.

8
STYLES AND MEDIA OF ILLUSTRATION
✝✝ ⏱90

Teaching content

Developing awareness of different styles of illustration.

What you need

A selection of books with a variety of illustration styles (including those provided in the workshop), photocopiable page 161.

What to do

Explain that some books are written and illustrated by the same person (author–

illustrators) and others are written by an author and illustrated by an illustrator. Most illustrators can work in several different styles (how they draw) and media (what they use to draw with), but tend to have one style that they prefer.

Give each pair a copy of photocopiable page 161. This contains a table to be completed. Ask the children to look through the selection of books and to find examples of, say, eight different illustration styles. They should record the title of each book and the name of the illustrator on the photocopiable sheet and tick the elements of style that apply.

Finally, the children should choose one of the books on their list and try to find other books by the same illustrator. Are the illustrations the same, or does the illustrator use different styles?

SHAPE AND LAYOUT OF ILLUSTRATIONS

Teaching content
Developing awareness of shape and layout of illustration.

What you need
The nine books provided in the workshop, a variety of other story books with illustrations (various styles), photocopiable page 162.

What to do
Use the books provided in the workshop to show that the illustrations in books can be in any shape, size or form, can be in a variety of positions on the page and can occur anywhere in the text – they don't always need to be at the end of a chapter at the bottom of the page or in a rectangular box!

Explain that illustrations can be used to:
• tell the story;
• help the reader imagine the story;
• add detail to the story;
• make the page look attractive and interesting;
• make the story accessible by breaking it into parts;
• reduce the need for lengthy description by using pictures rather than words.

Give the children about 10 minutes to look through the workshop books and other illustrated books and find one page each that particularly appeals to them visually. Then, put them into groups of four and give them another 10 minutes to share and talk about their choices.

End the lesson by encouraging the children to try to be aware of some of these issues when they illustrate their own work. Photocopiable page 162 is a template that can be used by children to plan illustration space for any piece of writing. You might like to have multiple copies available for children to use when they wish.

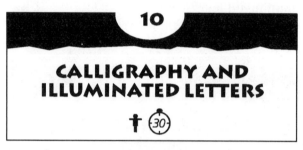

CALLIGRAPHY AND ILLUMINATED LETTERS

Teaching content
Introducing calligraphy and illuminated letters as techniques for presentation.

What you need
Photocopiable pages 163–166, photocopiable anthology page 212 (from *Aspects of the Craft of Writing*), pieces of card (approximately 18× 18cm), art materials including calligraphy pens and ink if available.

What to do
Create a display of calligraphy alphabets using some or all of photocopiable pages 163–165. Explain to the children that calligraphy is beautiful handwriting that can be used to liven up, decorate or add a professional finishing touch to their written work. Calligraphy can be simple or detailed depending on the effect you want to create and the materials you have available. If you do have the tools in the classroom, you might like to give the children some time to experiment with creating their own effects. Even with basic pens, ink and paper quite a number of styles and effects can be achieved.

Now, give each child a copy of photocopiable page 166 which shows a number of different styles of illuminated letters. Give them also copies of the anthology page which shows an illuminated letter being used to begin a passage.

Ask the children to look at the photocopiable pages and to choose the style they like best. They should then practise making their own

illuminated letters, perhaps starting with their own initials. If they prefer, they could make up a style of their own.

Now tell them that they are going to make a heading to go at the top of a display board. The heading should be long enough to allow each child in the class to produce a letter, for example: 'WELCOME TO CLASS XXX. HERE ARE SOME OF OUR STORIES.' Each child should then take responsibility for at least one letter and design an illuminated letter on a piece of card. Make sure the letters fill the card and that they stand out against the background design. They may have to be solid black to do this.

When all the letters are complete, put them together to make the heading. Although the children will probably have chosen a variety of styles to decorate their letters, the finished effect should be quite striking.

Now that the children have tried their hand at large illuminated letters, encourage them to use smaller versions, as on the anthology pages, when publishing their stories.

11

MAKING BORDERS

ᚋᚋ (35)

Teaching content
• Understanding that good presentation matters.
• Making effective border patterns.

What you need
A selection of published illustrated books with decorative borders, photocopiable anthology pages 203 and 212 (from *Aspects of the Craft of Writing*), photocopiable pages 167 and 168.

What to do
Show the children the decorative borders on the photocopiable anthology pages and others from the selection of published books. Point out that simple ideas can create beautiful effects. Carefully coloured chequered or striped borders can be very effective, as can borders with repeated logos or objects that are relevant to the story. Which borders do the children like best and why?

Talk to the children about the illustrator's choice of colours. Often a restricted range, complementary colours or shades of one colour can be very effective.

Give each group a copy of photocopiable pages 167 and 168 which contains a variety of border designs. Ask each child to select one pattern they particularly like and to explain to the rest of the group:
• what they like about it;
• if they were going to colour it, which colours they would choose and why.

Children can use the designs on this sheet as templates when publishing their own stories.

Explain that when children create their own borders, they must take care that the border is geometrically balanced on the page. However, they need not necessarily be parallel to the edges of the paper – some borders cover the corners of the page, rather like a photograph album.

12
TELLING THE WORLD
ʈʈʈʈʈ→ⓦ ⑳

Teaching content
• Examining ways of sharing writing with a wider audience.
• Developing sense of ownership and self-esteem.

What you need
Photocopiable page 169, a class with original published (or almost published) books that they want to share with a wider audience, chalkboard, writing materials.

What to do
Put the children into groups of six. Explain that now they have finished, or almost finished, their books, they will need to think about how to share their stories with a wider audience. Explain that authors and publishers have different ways of letting people know about recently completed books. Three important ways are:
• a book launch;
• a book reading;
• a book display.

For your purposes, each of these may be a low-key operation, involving only the class and one other class in the school, or it may involve work in the local library, invitations to other schools, parents, governors/school board members, PTA members and other friends of your school. It may be possible to time events to coincide with the school book week, a school fair, the opening of a new annexe, classroom or library, or another school celebration.

Each event has different characteristics and planning needs. Give out copies of photocopiable page 169 (one between two). This outlines the purpose and characteristic features of each of the events cited above. Read it through with the class and encourage the children to ask questions about each of the three events mentioned; it is important that everyone understands what each could involve.

Ask the children to discuss which way they think would be most appropriate and practical to inform others about the stories they have written. Explain that it is ultimately a teacher/class decision, but that you want to begin by

getting the children to think about the possibilities and hearing their views.

Tell each group to appoint a scribe (someone who can write quickly and legibly) and give them about 20 minutes to discuss and jot down the type and scale of event they would prefer and why.

To help, write the following aspects on the board for consideration:
• the time required for the actual event;
• the lead-in time to plan and prepare for the event;
• the amount of organisation and work involved (from the children and others);
• the number of people involved from outside the class/school;
• the specific attractions of each method;
• the nature of the stories and which event best suits the work.

After 20 minutes or so, bring the class together and make a joint decision about which publishing event you will go with on this occasion.

13

PLANNING THE EVENT

Teaching content
Planning a celebration of work.

What you need
Writing materials, large sheet of paper, marker pens, slips of paper (approximately 10 x 5cm).

What to do
The size and scale of your book event will depend very much on the circumstances of your children and school and what has happened in the past. Whatever the size of the operation, it must be carefully planned and prepared.

Discuss and list some of the things that will need to be done for the event, no matter what type it is. For example, the children will almost certainly have to:
• write to or ask the headteacher (and maybe other teachers) explaining what the book event is about and seeking permission;
• decide a date and time and place;
• book or reserve the venue;
• write invitations;
and so on.

Then ask the class to brainstorm specific things they might do and/or have at the book event they have chosen. Record these ideas on a large sheet of paper or the chalkboard. Ask each child to select and prioritise the three most important ideas, writing each idea on a separate piece of paper, using the numbers 1–3 to indicate the importance of each.

Put the children into groups of four and elect a chairperson for each group. It is this person's responsibility to ensure that all the ideas are discussed. The group must arrive at a joint decision about the four ideas they would most like to incorporate in the book event. These should be recorded by another group member, for presentation to the rest of the class.

Bring the class together for a final discussion/ negotiation and produce a (short) list of activities which will form the basis of the book launch. Be hard-headed during this discussion and spell out exactly how much work will be required for each idea/activity, along with the time available.

Write this final list on a large sheet of paper and display it somewhere in the classroom. Use numbers to indicate the order in which the activities/ideas will be implemented. Depending on how you choose to organise the class, you may also indicate which particular children or groups will be responsible for implementing particular ideas.

14

WRITING INVITATIONS

Teaching content
Functional writing.

What you need
Writing and colouring materials, chalkboard, list of people to be invited.

What to do
Explain to the children that they will need to write formal invitations to those who are to be invited to the book launch, reading or display of their most recently published books.

Ask the class to recall the important information on party invitations and list this on the chalkboard. Explain that, whereas almost everyone knows what a party is, not everyone

will know or understand what a book launch, reading or a display entails. The invitation must therefore also indicate what to expect (i.e. what people will be doing – listening to speeches, a story, reading the books, visiting a display...). Talk briefly about suitable layouts and designs before allocating, or allowing children to choose, someone for each of them to invite to the event.

15

ADVERTISING POSTERS

♦♦♦ ⏲20

Teaching content
• Developing awareness of important aspects of advertising posters.
• Making a poster.

What you need
Photocopiable page 170, for each child a story that he or she has published, poster-sized sheets of paper, writing and art materials, a camera (optional).

What to do
Before beginning the practical activity, review with the children the specific criteria for an advertising poster.

Then put the children into pairs and give each pair a copy of photocopiable page 170. Explain that this is a copy of an advertising poster for *A Lion at Bedtime*. Let the children examine the poster and discuss in their pairs the important elements of information given and evaluate the effectiveness of the design. Take a brief feedback from the class.

Ask the children each to plan and make an advertising poster for one of their own published stories. Alternatively, pairs could swap publications and create a poster for their partner's work. If the children wish to include a 'picture' of the book on their poster, the finished product could be photocopied and the copy coloured and stuck on to the poster – or a camera could be made available for photographs to be taken.

16

PRACTISING READING ALOUD

♦♦♦ ⏲20

Teaching content
Reading aloud with expression and meaning.

What you need
Children's own published books, photocopiable page 172, cassette recorder and blank cassette (if possible), photocopiable page 171 (optional).

What to do
The children must appreciate the importance of reading their stories aloud well. If their audience cannot hear or understand what they say, they will not appreciate the story. You must be prepared to give individual help to those with problems.

Explain that the children will need to practise reading their books aloud, and can help each other to do this well. First, let them read their book aloud to themselves. Then, ask them to read their stories to their writing partners, who should listen and make helpful comments on the reading using the response sheet on photocopiable page 172.

Development/homework task

Having read the advice from their writing partners, the children could record their stories and listen to their own performances, using the photocopiable sheet then for self-evaluation.

Some children may wish to offer a storytape as part of their publication. This package will be familiar to most children. Photocopiable page 171 offers a template for designing an inlay card for an audio cassette box.

17
READING THE STORIES

Teaching content
- Reading aloud with expression and meaning.
- Developing an awareness of audience.
- Developing self-esteem.

What you need
An audience, a child reader with his or her published book, photocopiable response sheet(s) accompanying the particular project, writing materials.

What to do
Book readings may be held in the school library, in a classroom or even in the local library if pre-arranged.

Spend some time explaining carefully to the children the importance of approaching their audience, whether they are old or young, with respect and kindness – that they must introduce themselves as the reader and author and thank the audience for coming to listen to the story. Suggest that the readers begin by showing the book, pointing out the illustrations and demonstrating any special features (if, for example, it stands up, has special pictures, opportunities for the listener to decide the storyline or paper-engineered moving parts). Point out that they may need to explain about the main character, or the setting.

Remind the children that, when they read their story, they should ensure that the listeners, particularly if they are young children, can see the writing and the illustrations. Finally, warn the readers to be prepared to let younger children touch the books, turning pages, opening doors and exploring the inside. Warn

them also that the listeners may want to hear the story a second time and that, as authors, they should be prepared to answer any questions their audience may have about their writing and publishing.

Finally, the photocopiable sheets that accompany each writing project can be used for listeners to record their responses to the story. If the listeners are other children, particularly young children, it is helpful if the teacher speaks to them about the amount of work and effort involved and the advantages of positive reviews. Whilst honesty in reviewing is desirable, it would be very easy to upset a tender young author and a balance must be kept in this area!

18
THE PUBLISHING PROCESS

Teaching content
Stages in the publication process.

What you need
Photocopiable pages 173–176, scissors, paper, glue.

What to do
Give each pair a copy of photocopiable pages 173 and 174 and explain that they contain a list of the main stages in the publishing process, but not in the correct order. Ask the children to cut out and place these stages into the sequence that they think would happen in the publishing process.

Then, give the children copies of photocopiable pages 175 and 176. These contain a description of the publishing process. Ask them to read this carefully and, in the light of this new information, to reconsider their original sequence for the stages.

When they are happy that the stages are in the right order, the children should stick the statements down on to a separate sheet of paper.

Development/homework task
With the help of other reference books, children can work in groups to add to and illustrate the information on the sheet, finally making this into a reference book on the publishing process.

THE COVER STORY

Cover features

Book title

Author's name

Illustrator's name

Publisher

Draw the publisher's logo here.

Price

ISBN

Does it have a 'blurb'? If so, does it make you want to read the book? Why?

Does it have quotes from the book or reviews? If so, write one of them out here.

What do you particularly like about this cover?

What would you suggest to make the cover better?

QUOTABLE QUOTES

◆ Use the forms below to record 'quotable quotes' from the stories you read.

Book title: _____

Author: _____

Quotation:' _____

_____

_____

_____ ' from page _____

This quotation is important to the story because... _____

_____

_____

_____

- ✂ - -

Book title: _____

Author: _____

Quotation:' _____

_____

_____

_____ ' from page _____

This quotation is important to the story because... _____

_____

_____

_____

BEYOND THE COVER

Title of book _____ Name of author _____

◆ Tick if your book has the following features:

	title page		list of author's other books
	dedication		list of other books in series
	author information		contents
	publisher's address		acknowledgements
	year of publication		index
	a copyright sign		

◆ Can you find the answers to the following questions in your book?
(You may not be able to find them all!)

1. If there is a dedication, who is the book dedicated to?

2. When was the book published?

3. Who has copyright of the text?

    Who has copyright of the illustrations?

4. In what year was the book first published?

5. What is the publisher's address?

6. Does the author thank (acknowledge) anybody. If so, whom?

7. Where was the author born?

8. Name one other book the author has written.

9. Name another book in the series or by the same publisher.

PUBLISHING GRAPHICS

About the author

© Copyright

Contents

I dedicate this book to
_____

Pictures by

Other stories by the same author:

Words by

Acknowledgements

What the reviewers say:

ABOUT THE AUTHOR

Name of author _____

Question 1 _____

Answer _____

_____

_____

Question 2 _____

Answer _____

_____

_____

Question 3 _____

Answer _____

_____

_____

Question 4 _____

Answer _____

_____

_____

Question 5 _____

Answer _____

_____

_____

Scholastic
IMAGINATIVE WRITING
Workshop

STYLES AND MEDIA OF ILLUSTRATION

◆ Try to find eight different styles of illustration in your selection of books. Then complete the table below, ticking the illustration features that apply for each book.

Book title	Illustrator	realistic	cartoon	sketch	comic strip	black and white	colour	watercolour	crayon

◆ Choose one of the books on your list and try to find other books by the same illustrator. Are the illustrations the same or does the illustrator use different styles?

SHAPE AND LAYOUT OF ILLUSTRATIONS

The outlines on this page can be used as illustration shapes for your story.

CALLIGRAPHY

A · B · C · D · E · F

G · H · I · J · K · L

M · N · O · P · Q

R · S · T · U · V

W · X · Y · Z

a · b · c · d · e · f g · h · i · j · k · l · m · n

o · p · q · r · s · t · u · v · w · x · y · z

CALLIGRAPHY

A B C D E F G
H I J K L M N
O P Q R S T U
V W X Y Z
a b c d e f g h i j k l m n
o p q r s t u v w x y z

CALLIGRAPHY

ABCDEF
GHIJKL
MNOPQ
RSTUV
WXYZ

ILLUMINATED LETTERS

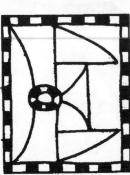

Scholastic
IMAGINATIVE WRITING
Workshop

BORDERS

◆ These can be copied and used by the children to decorate their books. From this master page, individual design masters can be made by pasting 5 or 6 copies of each design on a page.

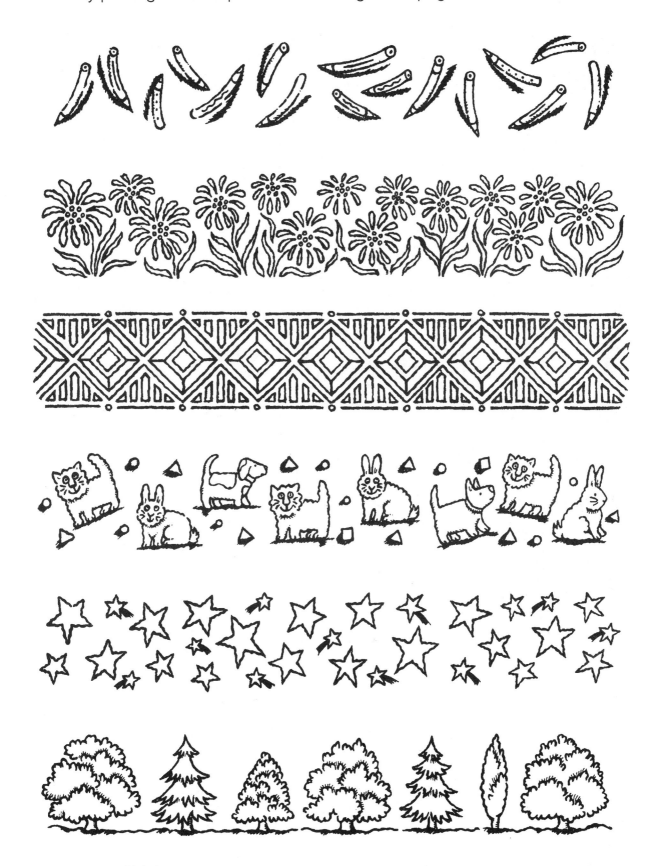

BORDERS

◆ These can be copied and used by the children to decorate their books. From this master page, individual design masters can be made by pasting 5 or 6 copies of each design on a page.

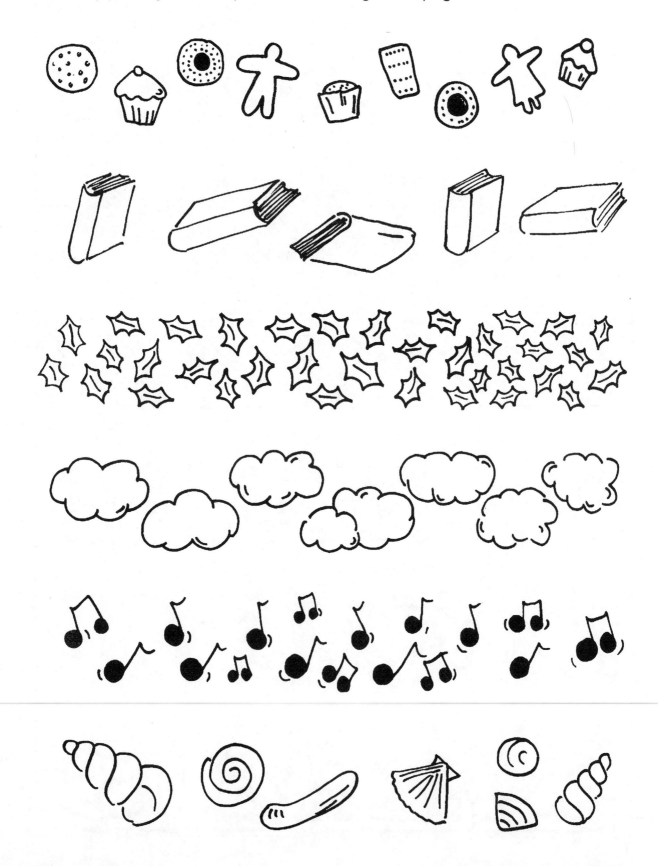

TELLING THE WORLD

	Purpose	Characteristics
A book launch	Visitors talk to writers and view and review new books.	Books are displayed. A special guest is invited – perhaps a local writer or journalist. Other guests are invited – parents/ senior citizens/school neighbours. Refreshments are provided. Two of the new books are featured prominently and volunteers make speeches about the authors and introduce their books.
A book reading	The books are introduced to a selected audience and read aloud by the authors.	Books are read to small groups from other classes in the school. A comfortable place is prepared for the audience. One author is selected to present their book in assembly. Children practise their book reading at home, which is evaluated by a family member. The children in the audience fill out an evaluation form.
A book display	Books are prominently displayed and visitors are given an opportunity to talk with the authors.	A local librarian visits the school to choose books for the display. Parents/local organisations are invited. Children make and give away/sell bookmarks. Visitors meet and talk to authors. Children hold book-making workshops and teach visitors how to make a particular type of book. Visitors are interviewed about their favourite books. The results of this are collated and later sent to the visitors.

PRESENTATION

A LION AT BEDTIME

DEBI GLIORI

'delightful ... another winner from Scholastic!'

SCHOLASTIC

AUDIO CASSETTE INLAY CARD TEMPLATE

Audio cassette

a reading of

by

Audio cassette

a reading of

by

PRACTISING READING ALOUD

Name of reader _____

Mark these questions on a scale of 1 to 5. Circle the number.

1. Excellent   2. Very good   3. Good   4. Not very good   5. Terrible

Was the story well introduced?	1	2	3	4	5
Was the story read clearly?	1	2	3	4	5
Could you hear every word?	1	2	3	4	5
Was it read at the correct speed?	1	2	3	4	5
Was the story read with expression?	1	2	3	4	5
Did the reader pay attention to punctuation?	1	2	3	4	5
Did the reader use different voices for different characters?	1	2	3	4	5
Did the reader make eye contact with the audience occasionally?	1	2	3	4	5
Did the reader stop to show the illustrations?	1	2	3	4	5

One good piece of advice to help the reader is _____

Signed by reader _____

Signed by partner _____

Scholastic
IMAGINATIVE WRITING
Workshop

THE PUBLISHING PROCESS (1)

1. The author has an idea.

The manuscript is marked up for printing and sent for typesetting into proofs.

The designer designs the cover, decides how the inside of the book will look and, in consultation with the author and editor, chooses an illustrator.

The author and editor read the proofs and correct any mistakes.

The book is sold to bookshops by the sales people and orders sent out from the warehouse.

An editor reads the manuscript and thinks it's brilliant. It is discussed at a publishing meeting, accepted and a contract agreed with the author.

The author writes the rest of the story and sends it to the editor.

The author writes part of the story and sends the manuscript to a publisher.

The designer prepares rough layouts, showing the position of text and illustrations.

THE PUBLISHING PROCESS (2)

The book is bought by the customer and read!

The publicity department decides how to publicise the book.

The paste-up goes off to the printer for film to be made and final proofs are sent back to the publisher for checking by the editor and designer.

When the artwork for the illustrations is done, the designer produces a final paste-up showing exactly how the text and illustrations fit on each page.

The editor edits the story, discussing it with the author as necessary, and checks for correct spelling, punctuation and grammar.

The book is printed and bound and all copies sent to the publisher's warehouse for storage.

The illustrator sends rough drawings to the publisher for approval.

Scholastic
IMAGINATIVE WRITING
Workshop

THE PUBLISHING PROCESS (3)

A book starts with an idea. Often it is an author who suggests the idea to a publisher. Sometimes, though, a publisher has the idea and asks an author to write it. And sometimes it is the illustrator who has the initial idea! All published books, however, are the product of many people working cooperatively.Although each publishing company may organise the work in a slightly different way, the process is similar.

Once the idea has been thought of, the author writes an outline and perhaps part of the story and sends it to a publisher, hoping that it will be accepted. An editor evaluates it and, if he likes it, proposes at a meeting that it be published. The proposal is discussed, accepted and a contract agreed with the author, saying what she will write and how she will be paid for her writing.

The author writes the rest of the story, drafting and re-drafting until she has a final version that she is happy with. She then sends it to the editor. He edits the story, discussing it with the author and perhaps sending parts of it back for reworking, if he feels that changes are necessary. Finally, he checks for correct spelling, punctuation and grammar.

The editor then meets with the designer to brief her, explaining what the book is about and what format it should have. The designer suggests ideas for the cover and how the inside of the book should look – for example, what typeface and typesize should be used and what style of illustration would be appropriate. In consultation with the author, editor and sales people, a final design is agreed and a suitable illustrator chosen.

THE PUBLISHING PROCESS (4)

The editor marks up the manuscript for printing and gives it to the production department who sends it off to a typesetter for setting into proofs. When the proofs are returned, the author and editor read them and correct any mistakes. The designer uses the proofs to prepare rough layouts, showing the position of the text and how much space is allowed for illustrations. These are sent to the illustrator who makes rough pencil drawings of the illustrations first for the publishers' and author's approval.

The publicity department uses all the information available to prepare information about the book and to plan how the book will be publicised and celebrated when it is published.

When the final artwork for the illustrations is done, the designer produces a paste-up showing exactly how the corrected text and finished illustrations fit on each page. This paste-up is given to the production department who sends it to the printer for the film to be made. The film is sent back to the publishers as ozalid proofs for a final check before printing plates are made.

The book is printed and bound and all the copies are sent to the publishers' warehouse for storage. When the sales people sell the book to bookshops, the orders go to the warehouse and the books are sent out from there.

The book is then bought by the customer and read – hopefully with a great deal of enjoyment!